YOUR NEXT BIG

IMPROVE YOUR CREATIVITY AND PROBLEM-SOLVING

Principal Editor: Ameesha Green
Editor: Ashley Strosnider
Proofreader: Janina Lawrence
Book and Cover Designer: David Miles

Some graphic elements used with permission from Shutterstock.com artists as follows: KanokpolTokumhnerd, Lukas Gojda, wenchiawang, Franzi, dastagir, CKURAT, F-dor, lineartestpilot, Drk_Smith, Aleksandra Novakovic, kkoman, mhatzapa, Visual Generation, Aleks Melnik, Ecelop, Angeliki Vel, BeatWalk, hchjjl, whitemomo, olessya.g, luma Kirau, MicroOne, Tupungato, Rawpixel.com, Nikolaeva, YasnaTen, Creative Stall, bsd, blue67design, ANNNA U, Sararoom Design, VikiVector, paramouse, Sko Olena, mhatzapa, Shizayats, dimpank, advent, KenshiDesign, Kristiana Budkevica, puruan, Erica Truex, rudall30, Zubdash, TabitaZn, Megarupa, olllikeballoon, Mumemories, Africa Studio, nata_fler, Song_about_summer, Supacharapong Buanark, sauletas, Stas Walenga, David Lee, VectorsArt, PedroNevesDesign, Sudowoodo, Carodejnice, richardwibi, artnLera, Kovalov Anatolii, Ekaterina Zimodro, Yoko Design, Vera Serg, Nata Kuprova, Taty Vovchek, zizi_mentos, tofutyklein, sailormoon, Babka, Freud, Ksenia Lokko, Valeriya Novozhonova, Antoniu, puruan, Dooder, olnik_y, AZdesign, hudhud94, phipatbig, and Benn Beckman.

Library of Congress Control Number: 2020906676
ISBN 978-1-7349130-0-2 (full-color version)
ISBN 978-1-7349130-2-6 (grayscale version)
ISBN 978-1-7349130-1-9 (e-book)

First edition

Published in Washington, District of Columbia
Printed in the United States

www.yournextbigideabook.com

YOUR NEXT BIG

Idea

by **SAMUEL SANDERS**

IMPROVE YOUR CREATIVITY AND PROBLEM-SOLVING

CONTENTS

Your Big Idea Journey Map 7

Introduction 9

Section 1: Identifying Problems, Needs, Wants, and Questions 19

CHAPTER 1: Identifying Problems 21

CHAPTER 2: Identifying Needs and Wants 29

CHAPTER 3: Asking Questions.. 39

CHAPTER 4: Why?... 55

CHAPTER 5: The Why 3x Rule 61

CHAPTER 6: What Inspired That? 67

Section 2: Erasing Stigmas... 75

CHAPTER 7: Defining a Stigma 77

CHAPTER 8: Finding and Erasing Stigmas in Practice........ 87

CHAPTER 9: Erasing Stigmas through Play 107

CHAPTER 10: Stigma Strategies... 117

CHAPTER 11: Erasing Long-Held Stigmas 123

CHAPTER 12: Challenging the Status Quo.......................... 129

Section 3: Creating Solutions 135

CHAPTER 13: There's No Such Thing as a Crazy Idea 137

CHAPTER 14: Brainstorming and Mind Mapping............. 147

CHAPTER 15: Selecting Solutions... 157

CHAPTER 16: Combining Solutions..................................... 163

Section 4: Feasibility Check 171

    CHAPTER 17: The Feasibility Check 173

Section 4.1: Personal Idea Feasibility Check 175

    CHAPTER 18: Do You Want to Pursue It? 177

    CHAPTER 19: What Is Stopping You? 187

Section 4.2: Business Idea Feasibility Check............................. 191

    CHAPTER 20: Is There a Market for the Idea?.............................. 193

    CHAPTER 21: Does the Market Want It *Now?* 201

    CHAPTER 22: Resources... 209

Section 5: Share, Share, Share 217

    CHAPTER 23: The Benefits of Sharing 219

    CHAPTER 24: It's Okay to Share.. 227

Section 6: So, What Now?... 235

    CHAPTER 25: Planning the Solution 237

    CHAPTER 26: Hacking Your Brain.. 245

    CHAPTER 27: A Run-Through of the Entire Process...................... 259

    CHAPTER 28: Make It Happen 265

    CHAPTER 29: What Next?... 275

Congratulations and Thank You! 279

YOUR BIG IDEA JOURNEY MAP

1 START
➡️ I'm ready to go ....GO TO 2

2 ASK QUESTIONS AND IDENTIFY PROBLEMS, NEEDS, AND WANTS
➡️ I have completed asking questions and discovering, and have identified a problem, need, or want........GO TO 3

3 FIND AND ERASE STIGMAS (USE STIGMA-FINDING AND ERASING STRATEGIES)
➡️ I still don't have a good enough understanding of my problem, need, or want to find and erase stigmas......................GO TO 2
➡️ I have found and erased stigmas, and I am ready for brainstorming and mind mapping.....................GO TO 4

4 BRAINSTORMING AND MIND MAPPING
➡️ I have brainstormed, and I need to go back to the drawing board based on my results...................GO TO 2
➡️ I need to go back and relook at finding and identifying my stigmas...............................GO TO 3
➡️ I have brainstormed, and I am ready to move forward to a solution.............................GO TO 5

5 COMBINE AND SELECT SOLUTIONS
➡️ I need to go back and brainstorm further to get the best solutions..............................GO TO 4
➡️ I have my solution! ....GO TO 6

6 THREE-PART FEASIBILITY CHECK
➡️ After completing my feasibility check, I realize this is not feasible...............................GO TO 2
➡️ After completing my feasibility check, I realize I need to re-evaluate my stigmas.................GO TO 3
➡️ After completing my feasibility check, I need to re-evaluate my idea..................................GO TO 4
➡️ After completing my feasibility check, I need to relook at the solution I selected.........................GO TO 5
➡️ My idea passes the feasibility check....................................GO TO 7

7 SHARE
➡️ After talking to people, I need to go back to the drawing board..............................GO TO 2
➡️ After talking to people, I need to re-evaluate my stigmas ....GO TO 3
➡️ After talking to people, I need to go back to my brainstorming stage ....GO TO 4
➡️ After talking to people, I need to relook at my feasibility check..............................GO TO 6
➡️ I am ready to go! ....GO TO 8

8 YOUR NEXT BIG IDEA! IT'S TIME TO MOVE FORWARD.

INTRODUCTION

T
hink of someone innovative, creative, elite at problem-solving, and excellent at ideation (that is, the ability to come up with ideas without tons of effort). You probably know people like this, but if not, then imagine someone. Do you ever wonder how people can get so good at those four skills? Have you ever told yourself "I'm just not creative or innovative—and that's just how it is"? Or maybe you think you're not good at coming up with ideas or solving problems in unique ways. Even if you think you're good at coming up with ideas, being creative, solving problems, and being innovative, perhaps you want to take your skills from good or great to elite.

Everything starts with an idea. Whether it's life-changing decisions or money-making products or processes—all successful decisions and companies begin with someone's idea. I've made it my business to study where these successful ideas come from and how to generate more of them. In my work life and my time as an entrepreneur, and in my personal life as a curious person, I've consistently found that the more ideas I consider, the better, and the same goes for most people. Some of the world's best ideas came from people who had previously come up with idea after idea after idea. A multitude and variety of ideas help me make critical decisions about where to focus my energy. Since I started practicing, I have consistently been able to come up with more than 100 ideas a week. This process of idea generation, which I will share with you in this book, has helped me move forward in my career. I hope it does the same for you.

I have founded multiple companies in my career, and these tactics for generating more ideas have been especially helpful in my professional life. At its peak, one company I co-founded, Wundershirt, sold athletic training clothing to Olympic athletes prepping for the 2016 Olympics. The same ideas we'll work through in this book helped me identify a problem that professional athletes faced—clothing does not help to improve athletic performance—and come up with an idea I thought could solve it—clothing using responsive nanofabric textiles to help athletes with performance. From there, I used many of the tactics detailed in this book to identify the resources I had and the ones I'd need to make the idea a reality. During my startup growth process, I was part of multiple incubators and watched founders from all over the world come up with ideas and solutions to problems, and I continued to learn from them the whole time.

Founding my own companies was exciting, but so was working with and learning from others. I was part of one of the *Inc.* 5000 fastest-growing companies, where I worked on their research and development team, developing new offerings. At this fast-growing company, I saw how ideas came to be and how problems were handled by a successful small business team. I also worked in business development for a Fortune Future 50 and Fortune 500 company. There, I saw how a large corporation approaches creativity, problem-solving, ideation, and innovation.

But my experience is not just about me. Throughout my career, I have been lucky to observe some of the best minds at all levels of business. This book brings together the knowledge I have gained from my personal development and professional life. I want to share this knowledge and experience here to help you master your creativity, problem-solving, ideation, and innovation.

Wherever you are on this journey of ideas, creativity, problem-solving, and innovation, this book is for you.

WHY IMPROVE THESE FOUR SKILLS?

Mastering these four skills will help you exponentially in both your career and your personal life. Being able to identify problems and come up with ideas to solve them in innovative and unique ways can transform your career. Whether you're an entrepreneur who wants to start a business and are looking for your next great idea, an employee looking to impress your manager to get a promotion, or an executive who wants to help you and your employees improve performance in the workplace, this book will guide you toward your goals.

However, being innovative, creative, good at solving problems, and an ace at coming up with ideas extends far beyond business. In your everyday life, you regularly face situations that require these skills. Whether it's small issues such as do-it-yourself projects, long-term issues such as building relationships, or one-off situations such as ethical dilemmas and family emergencies, these skills are vital. They mean you can look at problems in a new light and see your everyday life with a different mindset. When you apply these skills to your personal life, you can take the steps needed to reach your goals outside of your career, whether it's to improve your health and fitness, your friendships, or your quality of life.

When you master these four skills—innovation, creativity, problem-solving, and ideation—you can create wide-ranging benefits in your life. You can be more efficient as you come up with ideas to make your everyday life easier. You could advance your career or get a raise because of an innovation that puts your company ahead of the curve. You could even use these strategies to come up with the next big idea that changes the world. The possibilities are truly endless.

HOW DO YOU IMPROVE THESE FOUR SKILLS?

You're probably wondering how it's possible to improve these skills. Perhaps you think you're not naturally talented in these areas. The simple answer is: you can train your brain. Our ability to do something isn't limited or restricted to the things we can do now. We can learn. You can train your brain to expand beyond your current abilities.

This book will help you master the skills of innovation, creativity, problem-solving, and ideation by deeply examining how to come up with meaningful ideas. You'll find exercises and activities to train your brain regularly. We'll get your brain to the point where you will actively come up with meaningful, innovative, and creative ideas that can solve real problems.

By the end of the book, you'll be equipped with the skills to come up with **100 meaningful ideas** a week that you can apply to your career or personal life. You'll be able to produce innovative and creative solutions to problems you thought were unsolvable. These are what I like to call "game-changing ideas."

This book will take you through a step-by-step process to master those skills. We'll look at tactics and approaches to help you confidently:

1   Identify problems, needs, and wants, and ask questions
2   Erase stigmas
3   Solve problems
4   Check feasibility
5   Share, share, share
6   Move from idea to reality

YOU CAN COME UP WITH 100 IDEAS A WEEK

Have you done the math? That's more than 14 ideas a day. That's more than one idea every two hours. It might sound ambitious, overwhelming, or even crazy, but believe it or not, with a little training and practice, you can come up with 100 game-changing ideas a week.

In college, I took a class centered around idea creation, specifically finding feasible business and startup ideas. At the end of the first day, the professors announced, "Every week, you'll need to post 15 business ideas to a blog. This regular homework will make up a large part of your grade." The entire class gasped and immediately fired back: "15 a week—that's so many! How do you even come up with that many ideas? That's not fair. That's so hard!" My professors were surprised, but all the same, they told the class it was a requirement. This idea creation was necessary.

I was taken aback. I did the math. *That's more than two a day. I'm reasonably creative, but that is a lot of ideas.* I started off with ideas I'd come up with before the class started, but by week three, I was rapidly running out of ideas. It seemed like most of the class was struggling too. So I decided that instead of thinking of ideas, I should try to change my mindset to let the ideas come to me.

It worked, and it made me realize that we're often looking at idea creation all wrong. In that class, I started a strategy for idea creation. Over many years of practice, I continued to develop and perfect this strategy. In this book, I'll show you the strategy I use every day and the way of thinking I followed to become a master at letting ideas come to me. If you apply these strategies, you'll find you can easily come up with 100 ideas a week too.

I'll challenge you to apply these ideas to improve your everyday life, your job, company, projects, or school. However, it's not just about applying the ideas. The process of thinking up new ideas will keep your brain sharp. It enables you to evaluate and think through processes or create things that don't exist yet. You'll also become a better problem solver because your brain will adapt to identifying problems and working out solutions. This book isn't just about coming up with ideas. It's about challenging the way you currently think and getting you to think differently for the rest of your life.

WHO IS THIS BOOK FOR?

This book is for anyone who wants to improve these four key skills—ideation, creativity, problem-solving, and innovation—whether it's in your personal life or your career. When we talk about career and business ideas, they don't have to relate to a specific job. If you don't currently have a job, you can apply it to the job application process. If you're a homemaker, you can apply your ideas to your home. If you're a student, then every time we talk about business or careers, imagine we're talking about your school or learning experience or what you plan to do for a career. This book works best if you relate it to *your* personal experience.

WHAT DO YOU NEED TO GET STARTED?

This book is intended to be a practical workbook, so I encourage you to do the exercises as you read. That way, you'll really train your brain.

- Throughout this book, you'll find gaps to write your answers or draw images, so forget the old rule that "you can't write in a book!"
- Alternatively, you can use a notebook to do the exercises.

You're going to need a notebook for your future ideas anyway. Make sure you have easy access to it, so whenever you think of a new idea, you can write it down. The brain forgets quickly, so it's critical that you have a place to keep your thoughts, ideas, and processes to make sure you don't lose them.

Don't just limit your notebook to things mentioned in this book though. Anything that can develop your ideas belongs in the notebook, so use it to bring your ideas to reality and keep track of your thoughts.

If it's impractical to carry your notebook, you can write ideas down using your phone, but make sure you back your phone up regularly or copy the ideas out into your notebook. When it comes to brainstorming and making charts, a notebook is often better because it's more visual.

So here's your first mission: Get a pencil, eraser, and notebook. You'll need this to write down your ideas, solve problems, draw pictures, and jot down your messy thoughts. Your sensory memory only lasts a couple of seconds, and your short-term memory only lasts a couple of minutes. Science suggests we have at least 50,000 thoughts a day. So, if you have a good one, you're going to want to write it down. Use your notebook as you work through this book, and make it a habit. Write down anything and everything you think may help you.

Next, you need something a little less tangible. You need an open mind. If you're not willing to try the exercises or consider the ideas, you will never get to the point where you can come up with game-changing ideas. Having an open mind also means being critical, because being critical is an important part of this process. However, you shouldn't shut out ideas before you evaluate them.

Ready? Let's see what you've got.

EXERCISE 1:
ANY IDEA

Instructions: In your notebook, write down an idea you have. It can be any idea, whether it's silly or useful, a business concept, or something for your personal life. The goal is not to come up with a great idea, but to show yourself that you have the capability to come up with ideas. It can literally be any idea. Just write it down to get going. You don't need to do anything with it.

Conclusion: Congratulations! You just completed your first task. That wasn't so hard, was it? This task is purely to get your mind flowing and give you an easy goal to accomplish. The first step in becoming better at ideation, problem-solving, creativity, and innovation is doing small exercises like this to train your brain. As you work through the book and complete the exercises, you'll find that they come more naturally to you.

IDENTIFYING PROBLEMS, NEEDS, WANTS, AND QUESTIONS

CHAPTER 1

IDENTIFYING

PROBLEMS

When you see people come up with great business or life ideas, you may chalk it up to luck or natural creativity, but there's a process to coming up with ideas that are beneficial to yourself and society. The first step in the process is to notice problems. Humans are routine beings, so we may face problems every day without even thinking twice about them. Some of us are very observant, and some of us are not. I'm going to challenge you to dig deep and look for everyday problems that you and others face. Once you're able to identify these problems, they will provide a basis for idea creation.

Analyze everything you're doing, even right at this moment. Think about all of the negative thoughts you have. Are your eyes tired from reading? You don't feel like making dinner? Maybe you're waiting on hold on a phone call. Those are all problems. A **problem** is defined as the intermediate point stopping you getting from your current situation to your ideal situation. Every day, we hear the words "can't" or "won't." A problem can even be an annoyance you feel—no matter how big or how small. When you're doing your next activity, think about all the problems you need to overcome to complete what you want to do. With every success, activity, or task, there are problems you need to overcome. What are they?

EXERCISE 2:

IDENTIFYING YOUR

FIRST PROBLEMS

Instructions: Now you're going to come up with problems. If you're looking to focus on your career and business, then centralize your problems around your career and industry. If you're looking to focus on just your personal life, then centralize your problems on personal situations. It's actually helpful to do both, because it's important to look at problems on both sides of your life. If you want to do both, then just split your list. Find some career-focused and some personal-focused problems.

Part 1: Write down three problems you had to overcome today while completing tasks, activities, or other commitments.

1 _____

2 _____

3 _____

The magic word for finding problems

There's a magic word for finding problems. When you hear it casually said about something, anything, it indicates a problem. That word is *hate*. How many times have you heard someone say, "I hate that…" or "I hate this…"? Hate means someone is facing a problem. Keep your ears open.

If someone hates that they have such a short lunch break, then a problem could be they "don't have enough time to eat" or "don't have enough time to relax after eating." Lots of problems can be configured by statements of dislike. Think about things you don't like or even hate. Then turn all of those dislikes or hates into problems or multiple problems. Finding problems is the first step in coming up with new ideas.

Part 2: Write down three more problems based on things you hate. If you hate something, form it into "a problem statement." For example, if the hate is: I hate hitting the snooze alarm too many times. The problem statement would be: "I have trouble waking up quickly in the morning, and as a result, I hit the snooze button too many times and start my day later then I would like to." While you're working, make sure you identify the problem *itself* and not just what is happening that made you notice the problem in the first place. In this example, the snooze alarm isn't the actual problem here.

1 _____

2 _____

3 _____

An extra keyword you can look out for is *annoying*. If you or someone else finds something annoying, this can lead you to discover problems.

Part 3: Write down three more problems based on things you find annoying. Reword the annoyance, turning it into a problem statement.

1 _____

2 _____

3 _____

Problems aren't always easy to find on the surface level, but if you focus on specific areas of displeasure and listen to what people say, you'll be able to find plenty of problems in our everyday world. The more problems you find, the more ideas you will eventually be able to come up with to solve them! In the next exercise, you're going to consider someone's normal daily routine to identify everyday problems.

EXERCISE 3:

A MORNING IN

THE LIFE OF ALEX

Instructions: Read a story about Alex's morning, keeping an eye out for problems she's facing. Circle, highlight, or write down all of the problems you can find.

Alex wakes up in the morning and is still tired, so she snoozes her alarm. After the second snooze, she gets up, yawns, and stretches. She walks to her bathroom, but because it's dark, she accidentally bumps into a table nearby. She looks around for her toothbrush and grabs the toothpaste. There's not much toothpaste, so Alex pushes the toothpaste tube to slide out the remainder the best she can. She proceeds to brush her teeth and look at her phone to check her messages. She slowly opens her phone with one hand and reads her messages. She receives great news—one of her friends is inviting her to go camping this weekend. She can't remember whether she has plans, so she replies that she thinks she can go, but she needs to double-check.

She then gets dressed, leaves her apartment, and walks to the subway for work. She stops and waits for cars to pass as she goes between city blocks. She gets to the subway and fumbles through her wallet, looking for her card to get in. She finds it and swipes in. As she's waiting for the subway, she notices a man playing music with a sign saying, "Free professional lessons, call (718) 718-7188," but he doesn't seem to have any traction. She catches the subway, and because it's morning rush hour, it's packed. She rides some stops and wants to check how many more stops until her destination. She can't find a sign, so she pulls out her phone and sees she has eight more stops. She eventually arrives, gets off the subway, and waits in line to leave the station.

Alex walks into the office and gets stopped on her way in by security to have her ID checked for clearance. She works on the 45th floor, so she gets in the elevator with 15 other people, and among them, they select eight different floors. She eventually makes it to her floor. She walks to her desk and sits down. She adjusts her chair and goes to log in to the computer. The computer takes a while to load

her password, but she logs in. She quickly checks the news and then
starts her workday.

Have you made your list? Let's take a look at an example list.

In just two hours of Alex's morning, we can identify multiple problems:

1   Alex is too tired in the morning.

2   Alex spends extra time snoozing her alarm.

3   Alex isn't stretched or loose when she wakes up.

4   Alex hits her table because her room is too dark.

5   Alex's toothbrush isn't easy to find.

6   Alex doesn't have an efficient way of getting out the rest of her toothpaste.

7   Alex goes through her phone slowly, because she only has one free hand while brushing her teeth.

8   Alex doesn't have an active schedule ready, so she can't get back to her friend with the answer.

9   Alex has to walk and take the subway, which is time consuming.

10 Alex has to stop at crosswalks, wasting more time.

11 Alex doesn't have her subway card readily available.

12 The man playing music can't seem to get people to stop and take down the number to have lessons with him. (It's important to not just focus on one person or on yourself, but to notice other people's problems too.)

13 The subways are too crowded.

14 There is no signage on the subway to show which stops are next.

15 Alex has to wait in line to get out of the subway.

16 Alex needs to stop her flow to get her ID checked on the way into work.

17 Alex has to wait a long time in the elevator for everyone else to get off on their floors.

18 Alex's chair isn't readily adjusted for her.

19 Alex's computer is not ready for her.

20 Alex's computer takes a long time to load.

Conclusion: These are not the only problems that can be found in this story. If you've found more, then good job! Extra bonus points if you picked up the problem with the man offering lessons. It's important to analyze your problems, but it's just as important to notice the problems others are facing. As you can see, from just two hours in someone's day, we came up with 20 problems and possibly more. As you'll learn later, every problem has multiple solutions. So, this simple story can lead to lots of ideas.

This is the mindset you need to put yourself in as you go through your everyday life. You need to be able to identify problems in order to come up with productive ideas. I challenge you now to do this for your workday or weekend—or ask a friend about their workday and identify potential problems. You can even pick up a book and analyze the problems a character is facing.

The only way to get better at identifying problems is to *practice.* With practice, the ability to find problems will become natural to you. The more problems you can find, the better. When finding problems, it's important to think of each of them as a *potential opportunity!* Each problem will provide you with a new chance to come up with a lot of ideas. Later, we'll look at how to turn these problems into game-changing ideas, but for now—keep practicing, and this will become a natural process for you.

CONCLUSION

Being able to take a step back and look at what you've overcome is the first step in idea creation. The second step is starting to identify problems all around you in everyday life—problems you probably hadn't noticed before because they were hidden behind words like "hate" and "annoying." Additionally, they can be things that have become so routine you haven't noticed they're problems.

Understanding and identifying problems is crucial to your success in coming up with 100 ideas a week and becoming more innovative, more creative, better at problem-solving, and better at ideation. So, congratulations. You're one step closer to achieving your goals!

CHAPTER 2

IDENTIFYING NEEDS AND WANTS

In the previous chapter, we looked at identifying problems as a way to help form ideas. In this chapter, we'll see how identifying needs or wants can also help to form ideas. If people need something they don't have—or they want something they don't have—then this is a potential opportunity to generate ideas to solve these needs and wants.

IDENTIFYING NEEDS

A **need** is something a person feels they should have because it's important or is a requirement. We need certain things to function, such as water, air, and sleep. I call these *functional* needs. These needs apply to everyone. However, needs can be a little broader than functional needs and can differ depending on the person. Some people need to have more friends than others to be happy. Some people need to have a car to get to work. While some needs are functionally necessary, other nonfunctional needs can be just as important to a person. They can feel as necessary to that person as water or air. I call these needs *auxiliary* needs. These are needs that feel like a must to some people, but not to every single person. These needs also lead to ideas.

To spot a need, you can look out for the words *have to*. If someone says, "I have to do this" or "I have to have that," they're talking about a potential need. Keep your ears perked for this set of keywords. If someone has to watch a TV show every day, this is an auxiliary need. Habits can also form needs that feel just as real as actual survival needs.

Some needs may not even feel necessary at all. For example, if someone says they have to take out the garbage once a week when the garbage collection comes, this may not feel like a need, but if they do it every single week of the year, this will qualify as a need. Needs can also be things the person doesn't currently have, for example, if someone says, they "have to get a new job" or "have to get a pet."

The way you decide whether it's a need or not is by answering this question: if the person doesn't do this action or thing, will it make them unhappy, throw off their day, or negatively impact their mental state? If yes, then the habit is so ingrained in their life that it would qualify as a need for them. Everyone has their own set of needs. Not everyone has the same auxiliary needs. Not all needs are universal.

IDENTIFYING WANTS

Wants are things that people desire. Some people want a coffee, want to take a walk, or want to travel. Wants, while not as urgent as problems or needs, can lead to ideas and opportunities. To identify a want, the keyword to look for is *wish*. If someone wishes they had something or wishes something would happen, this is a want. Look out for people talking about desires or wishes, because that will lead you toward "want" conclusions.

ANALYZING NEEDS
AND WANTS

When analyzing needs and wants, make sure you look both internally (at yourself) and externally (at other people). It's important to realize what you want and need, but it's just as important to notice what other people want or need.

While we've considered them separately until now—problems, needs, and wants can be thought of together as a whole. Sometimes, you'll encounter a situation where the same problem can be written as a want, need, or problem. For example, if someone says they would be so much happier with a pet, this can be considered in all three ways:

1 **Problem:** This person does not have a pet.
2 **Need:** This person needs a pet.
3 **Want:** This person wants a pet.

Typically, I like to put these in the problem form, because it's easier to analyze something as a problem and often leads to a more creative solution, which is something we'll discuss later. There are some things you want but may not feel you need. However, whether you notice something as being a problem, a need, or a want, with a little thinking, you can reorganize it into either of the other two forms. This is important because sometimes it's easier to think of something in one way (as a need, for example), but in another situation, it might be easier to progress if you think about the statement as a problem. For example, you may notice that someone needs more sunlight in their bedroom in order to be happy. This is easy to identify as a need, but when trying to solve that need, it might be easier to look at it as a problem: "There is not enough sunlight in the bedroom." Then you can identify how to fix that problem.

EXERCISE 4:
NOAH AND WILLIAM
GO TUBING

Instructions: Read this story about Noah, keeping an eye out for what he wants and needs. I want you to circle, highlight, and write down all of the needs and wants you can find.

Noah wakes up in the morning and jumps out of bed with excitement because he's going water tubing today. He goes to check whether his brother William is awake yet, but he's not. Noah heads downstairs, deciding he should have a good meal before being out on the water for the day. He checks the fridge for eggs, but he can't find any, so he gets in his car and drives down the road to the store. Knowing he's short on time, he looks for eggs quickly and purchases extra food for William.

He heads back home and immediately begins to cook the eggs. William walks downstairs and rubs his stomach, indicating he's hungry as he stares at the food. Noah knows they have to be ready on time or everyone will leave without them, so he cooks quickly. They eat and discuss how excited and lucky they are to be going tubing. They finish their breakfast and leave their dishes in the sink since there isn't much time.

"Noah, you need to drive," William says, "I'm not quite awake yet." Noah laughs, hops in the car, and drives to the local coffee shop, picks up two coffees, and then continues to drive to the lake. When they arrive, Noah and William head to the desk in the tubing shack to check in. The guide hands them papers to sign, along with safety and requirement warnings. William and Noah see that there is a record of two people holding on without falling out of the tube: 8 minutes and 16 seconds. They decide to try to break that record.

They board the boat, which takes them to the middle of the lake. Once there, they swim out in the cold water to the tube. They scramble on, and the tubing begins! After a few minutes of holding on, Noah yells to William asking whether he knows how much time has passed. William says he's not sure. Noah's hands start to slip, and he's not sure how much longer he'll last. The boat then takes a sharp turn, and Noah goes flying like a rock skipping on water. He swims back to the tube, letting everyone know he's okay and wishing he could have held on for longer.

Have you made your list? Let's take a look at an example list.

From just a few hours of this story, I've listed 15 needs or wants:

1   Noah wants to know whether his brother is awake.

2   Noah needs to have a good meal before doing water activities.

3   Noah wants his fridge to be stocked with food.

4   Noah wants to find grocery items quickly because they don't have much time.

5   William wants food as soon as he wakes up.

6   Noah wants to speed up his cooking time.

7   Noah and William need to get to their tubing appointment on time.

8   Noah and William want to talk about tubing.

9   Noah and William want their dishes to be clean, but they don't have time to wash them.

10 William needs Noah to drive because he's not awake.

11 The guide needs William and Noah to manually sign forms before they can go. (Bonus points if you spotted someone else's need besides the two main characters.)

12 William and Noah want to break the record for longest time without falling.

13 William and Noah need to swim to the tube in the middle of the lake to start.

14 Noah and William want to know how much time has passed while they are tubing.

15 Noah wants to be able to hold on to the tube for longer.

Conclusion: If you wrote down more needs and wants than this list, that's great! Like with noticing problems, spotting needs and wants takes practice. Again, if you want to continue your practice, you can listen to stories from friends and others, analyze your own life, and even look at fictional characters to help you identify needs and wants. As you continue to practice, you'll start to see more and more needs and wants, which will lead to more ideas.

EXERCISE 5:
A BUSINESS CALL

Instructions: So, you've identified problems, needs, and wants separately. Now we're going to follow Bailey, who is joining a business call. See whether you can identify the problems, needs, and wants for this situation.

It's 11:02 a.m., and Bailey forgot he had a call with the offshore team. He's exhausted from his past few calls, but he quickly dials in and joins the call. Bailey wants to signify he has joined, but too many people are talking, so it takes a while. He finally hears a pause and says, "Hello, Bailey is on the line." He hears a "Hi, Bailey" from someone else on the call, and "We're still waiting for Aubrey because he had some questions related to marketing." There are ten people on the line. They wait another three minutes until Aubrey joins and says, "Sorry guys, the CEO held me. Okay, let's get started."

Two people begin to speak at once, and then there is a pause. Then the two people begin to speak again, and there is another pause. Bailey hops in and says, "Aubrey, I hear you have some questions, but I was wondering whether you got those warehouse capacity numbers for me? I can't make any progress and need those numbers to continue." Aubrey replies that he will get the numbers and then begins asking marketing questions.

The meeting continues. Work is assigned as the meeting ends. Nine out of the ten people spoke. In the first ten minutes, three people spoke. In the second ten minutes, three different people spoke, and in the last ten minutes, three additional different people spoke.

Have you made your list? Let's take a look at an example list:

1   **Problem:** Bailey does not have a reminder for his call.

2   **Want:** Bailey wants to be less tired.

3   **Problem:** Bailey has no way to easily signify he has joined the call.

4   **Problem:** Everyone has to wait for Aubrey, wasting time (three minutes of 10 people's time means 30 combined minutes wasted).

5   **Problem:** There is no good way to decide who's speaking.

6   **Need:** Bailey is not getting the information he needs quickly enough for his job.

7   **Problem:** One person didn't speak on the call at all.

8   **Problem:** A lot of time was wasted since only three people were talking at a time.

Conclusion: Simple situations like a conference call can provide lots of problems, needs, and wants. Along with that, each individual on the call may have different problems, needs, and wants too. If you found more than are listed, that's fantastic! Additionally, if you listed something as a need or want but I have it as a problem above, or vice versa, that's good too. As long as you have the underlying issue listed. The better you're able to identify these problems, needs, and wants, the better you will be able to come up with game-changing ideas. Did you find this easier than the previous two exercises after some practice?

EXERCISE 6:
MONITORING YOUR FRIEND
OR A FICTIONAL CHARACTER

Instructions: Go and talk to a friend about their day or read a story about a fictional character. Write down as many problems, needs, and wants as you can find.

CONCLUSION

When you practice putting yourself in this mindset, you'll start to notice problems, needs, and wants more often in daily life, and it will come to you more naturally. Once you get into this mindset, you'll be able to identify an unbelievable amount of ideas to resolve them. This will lead to an increase in creativity, innovation, and problem-solving. Keep the practice going every day!

CHAPTER 3

ASKING
QUESTIONS

W hen you want to become more creative and innovative, it's important to *question everything*. Have you ever felt embarrassed to ask a question? You shouldn't be, because questions provide a foundation. They lay the groundwork for understanding information and are the very basics in information gathering and problem-solving. In this chapter, we'll go through five big questions (who, what, when, where, and how?) that are a crucial part of the process that leads to ideas.

WHY QUESTION THINGS?

There's a reason kids ask tons of questions. Questions help you grow—they fill knowledge gaps and are part of the learning process. They help you gather knowledge and understand information. Questions are a vital part of solving problems and creating ideas. Without asking questions, you'd never be able to take in the information you need to create new ideas. If we didn't question anything, we would just be robotically following instructions. If we choose not to ask a question, we could be missing vital information critical to solving the problem. Therefore, we need to keep asking them.

WHAT TO ASK

Imagine you're approaching a new situation. Before making any decisions, you want to gather more information. The first questions you're going to ask are:

1   What is happening in this new situation?
2   Who is involved in this new situation?
3   When did this new situation begin and when will it end?
4   Where is this new situation taking place?

Let's look at each type of question:

"What" questions provide us with information about the events and actions taking place. It's important to understand what is taking place, because this will lay the groundwork for finding problems, needs, and wants. If you're not aware of events, actions, or circumstances, then you're not going to find problems, needs, or wants in them. For example, let's say you need a place to stay, so you book a hotel room. You'll want to know what amenities it has. What is the name of the hotel? What is your room number? What do you need to show to complete the transaction? Understanding circumstances, events, and actions are the starting points in identifying problems.

"**Who**" questions identify the people involved in the situation. It's important to understand the stakeholders, that is, those who have something "at stake" in the problem—something to gain or lose. Knowing who is involved can determine the market for an idea or can help you understand who you shouldn't involve in an idea. It may indicate the best person to go to for advice about an idea or who may be able to help make your idea a reality.

"**When**" questions give you answers about timing. The timing of events, circumstances, or situations can make a real difference in their outcomes, and timing affects the stakeholders involved. It's important to understand when events may take place. You don't want to look for a full moon at 1:00 p.m., and you don't want to bother your CEO while they're on a call with the board of directors. Understanding the "when" in a situation is a critical step.

"**Where**" questions help you identify any location-related aspects. The location of an event is important because it helps you determine how the event will play out. It can hint who may be involved or what is happening. It may tell you which location you need to operate in to have the most successful ideas.

As you may have noticed, these types of questions are interconnected. In order to have a full understanding of the situation, you need to identify answers to all of these questions. Understanding these connections and learning about new situations can lead to many new ideas.

EXERCISE 7:
DAILY LIFE QUESTIONS

Instructions, Part 1: Write down 40 questions that pertain to your life using "who," "what," "when," or "where" (make 10 questions starting with each). For example, it could be, "Who is the leader of my division in my company?", "When does the sun officially rise near me?", "What is the craziest thing I can make for lunch using the food I have?", or "Where would my company expand to next if it was planning an expansion?"

These could be questions you have about work or life in general. If you want to focus on your personal life, that's fine. If you want to focus on your career, you can do that too, or you can do some of each. These could even be questions we don't know the answer to, such as, "What happens after we die?"

Have you made your list? Here are my 40 questions—10 who, 10 what, 10 when, and 10 where:

1   Who is the first person I usually talk to in the morning?

2   Who was the leader of Palau in 2000?

3   Who makes the decisions on the prices of flights?

4   If my family was going through a problem, who would be the first person to step up?

5   Who is the fastest Olympic swimmer ever?

6   Who holds the most Guinness World Records?

7   Who is the most recent pitcher to throw a perfect game in Major League Baseball?

8   Who is currently the oldest CEO of a Fortune 500 company?

9   Who has had the most number one *Billboard* hits of all time?

10 Who has the most popular name in the world?

11 What is the distance between Jupiter and Earth?

12 What is the first thing I would do if aliens were confirmed to be real?

13 What is the process for becoming a local mayor?

14 What are the ingredients in baumkuchen?

15 What is the most important aspect of friendship?

16 What is the reason I am writing this book?

17 What is the farthest distance I can kick a field goal?

18 What is the first picture that comes up when I search "cute cartoon armadillo"?

19 What is the meaning of life?

20 What would make me more tired: hopping like a bunny 20 times or skipping 20 times?

21 Where is the happiest country on earth?

22 Where can I go to trade stocks in South Africa's market?

23 Where would I go to find the scariest haunted house in the United States?

24 Where was the first basketball game played?

25 Where can I find the most Fortune 1000 and top 250 private company headquarters?

26 Where is the best place to get a scuba diving license?

27 Where would I go to see the closest professional Ultimate Frisbee game?

28 Where would I call home?

29 Where would I most like to travel next?

30 Where was the closest running trail to me growing up?

31 When was the first restaurant created?

32 When was the first taxi used?

33 When was the last time I texted someone I haven't seen in a while?

34 When is the best time to see the Northern Lights in Barrow, Alaska?

35 When is the best time to find wild lions in Zambia?

36 When did I go to bed last night?

37 When was the last time I stopped to meditate?

38 When was the light bulb invented?

39 When was coffee invented?

40 When did Babylon collapse?

It's important to take a step back and question things you may or may not know. We're so used to our daily patterns that we often don't have the freedom or time to ask questions about life. The more questions you come up with that you want an answer to, the more information you will have. And the more problems, needs, and wants you will notice, which will lead to more ideas. Asking questions is key to increasing ideation, creativity, innovation, and problem-solving.

You should also ask questions about a wide variety of topics, which will ultimately lead to more ideas because you're looking at a broader scope. This is what we'll look at next.

Part 2: Now that you've written down your questions, go and solve them. You may not have all of the answers, or you may need to go out and test them for yourself. Some questions may not have universally agreed-upon answers, and that's okay too. What's important is the learning, the process, and the habit of continually asking questions.

\\

Conclusion: The answer to my questions are (at the time of writing):

1   Who is the first person I usually talk to in the morning?
    After reviewing, it varies drastically based on the morning. I didn't find any patterns.

2   Who was the leader of Palau in 2000?
    In 2000, Kuniwo Nakamura was the president of Palau. He was the sixth president of Palau and started his presidency in 1993.

3   Who makes the decisions on the prices of flights?
    Airlines have computer systems that determine pricing.

4   If my family was going through a problem, who would be the first person to step up?
    After asking around, I came to realize that it can be drastically different depending on the nature of the problem. For example, if something was wrong with our home, my dad would be the first to inspect the issue.

5   Who is the fastest Olympic swimmer ever?
    Michael Phelps holds the title of the fastest swimmer. As of 2020, he has the most Olympic swimming records.

6   Who holds the most Guinness World Records?
    Ashrita Furman has set more than 700 world records and currently holds 200 of them.

7   Who is the most recent pitcher to throw a perfect game in

Major League Baseball?

As of the 2019 season, it is Félix Hernández.

8   Who is currently the oldest CEO of a Fortune 500 company?

As of 2020, it is Warren Buffett. Warren Buffet was born on August 30, 1930.

9   Who has had the most number one *Billboard* hits of all time?

According to Billboard, *The Beatles have 20.*

10   Who has the most popular name in the world?

According to the sixth edition of The Columbia Encyclopedia *(2000), Muhammad is probably the most common given name in the world, including variations.*

11   What is the distance between Jupiter and Earth?

According to the National Aeronautics and Space Administration (NASA), Jupiter is an average distance of 4.2 astronomical units away from Earth. One astronomical unit, is the distance from the Sun to Earth.

12   What is the first thing I would do if aliens were confirmed to be real?

After thinking about it, I would probably be excited and want to do additional research.

13   What is the process for becoming a local mayor?

I learned that each city is different, but each town should have a charter explaining what the process is.

14   What are the ingredients in baumkuchen?

Butter, eggs, flour, salt, sugar, vanilla and sometimes baking soda.

15   What is the most important aspect of friendship?

While there seems to be no definitive answer, I personally believe that care is the most important aspect.

16 What is the reason I am writing this book?
I would love to share my mindset of idea creation with people.

17 What is the farthest I can kick a football field goal?
Between 35 and 40 yards.

18 What is the first picture that comes up when I search "cute cartoon armadillo"?
An image of a small armadillo on all fours looking at me with big blue eyes.

19 What is the meaning of life?
There are many scientific and philosophical potential answers, but the real reason is unknown. Personally, I think there is not one single meaning and that life is up to interpretation according to the individual.

20 What would make me more tired: hopping like a bunny 20 times or skipping 20 times?
Hopping like a bunny.

21 Where is the happiest country on earth?
According to the World Happiness Report 2020, *it's Finland.*

22 Where can I go to trade stocks in South Africa's market?
The Johannesburg Stock Exchange, at the corner of Maude Street and Gwen Lane in Sandton, Johannesburg, South Africa.

23 Where would I go to find the scariest haunted house in the United States?
According to a 2019 survey by Hauntworld.com, the scariest haunted house in the United States is Headless Horseman's

Hayrides and Haunted Houses in Ulster Park, New York.

24 Where was the first basketball game played?

At a gym that was formerly on the grounds of Springfield College.

25 Where can I find the most Fortune 1000 and top 250 private company headquarters?

New York City.

26 Where is the best place to get a scuba diving license?

According to Lonely Planet's list of the top learn-to-dive locations, the best is the Gili Islands in Indonesia.

27 Where would I go to see the closest professional Ultimate Frisbee game?

I'm from Philadelphia, so the local team is the Philadelphia Phoenix of the AUDL, and they play in A. A. Garthwaite Stadium.

28 Where would I call home?

Philadelphia is the area where I've lived the longest.

29 Where would I most like to travel next?

South America.

30 Where was the closest running trail to me growing up?

The Radnor Trail.

31 When was the first restaurant created?

According to the Telegraph, *the first restaurant was created in 1765.*

32 When was the first taxi used?

The first modern taxi was used in London in August 1897.

33 When was the last time I texted someone I haven't seen in a while?

It was just two days ago.

34 When is the best time to see the Aurora Lights in Barrow, Alaska?

According to Alaska.org, any time between September 1 to April 20 is the best time.

35 When is the best time to find wild lions in Zambia?

The dry season is the best time to see wild animals, according to USA Today.

36 When did I go to bed last night?

12:56 a.m.

37 When was the last time I stopped to meditate?

Probably a few weeks ago.

38 When was the light bulb invented?

1879.

39 When was coffee discovered?

According to the National Coffee Association of the United States, there is no clear answer to where it was discovered, although many believe it was discovered in Ethiopia in the 11th century.

40 When did Babylon collapse?

539 B.C.

Information, knowledge, and experiences are key to coming up with ideas. You use what you know and what you have experienced to come up with solutions. This exercise was broad, but it's important to get in the habit of asking questions and getting curious about the answer to questions.

Sometimes, the more specific the topic, the easier it is to ask questions about it. If this exercise was challenging because it was broad, don't be discouraged. Go back and try to do it again about a specific subject. Later, you'll ask questions that are specific to work, school, or other important situations, which will lead to more ideas. Keep asking questions, and you will see these skills improve!

THE QUESTION "HOW?"

As you may have noticed, we haven't yet covered the last question from our list—"how." Unlike the other four big questions, **"how"** leads to *processes.* A lot of new ideas arise because there are problems with the way things are currently being done. So asking how something works may help you move toward an idea more directly than the other four questions.

"How" is perhaps the most unanswered question, even though really simple processes can be resolved with a "how" question. "How" questions give you deeper learning. Let's take a look at a simple process such as ordering a side dish of broccoli at a restaurant.

1 **What is it?** *It's broccoli.*
2 **Who made the broccoli?** *The chef.*
3 **When was it made?** *Probably a few minutes before it was served.*
4 **Where was the broccoli made?** *At the restaurant.*
5 **How was it made?** *The chef trimmed off the florets, then chopped them until the broccoli was in bite-size pieces. They took up a skillet and added oil, heating it on a medium to hot setting. The broccoli*

was dried then tossed in with a pinch of chopped garlic, salt, thyme, and basil. Lastly, it was placed in a serving bowl.

As you can see, "how" questions can lead to more information and longer conclusions than the other four questions.

EXERCISE 8:

HOW THINGS WORK

Instructions: Do you know the answer to the following basic "how" questions? If you don't, you can find the answers afterward, but try answering them first. Feel free to guess if you need to. When you're finished, come up with five more "how" questions you're interested in, and answer those too. (Again, feel free to ask "how" questions about your personal life, career, or both).

1   How does the internet work?
2   How does your body know when to burp?
3   How do you recycle old paper to use it again?
4   How does a vacuum work?
5   How does your body digest new food?

6   _____

7   _____

8   _____

9   _____

10 _____

Answers

1   How does the internet work?

Underground wires transfer files from one place to another. This is called a network. When multiple networks are connected, that's an internet network. But how do files get sent to specific devices or computers? Each computer has an Internet Protocol (IP) address. Each address has an IP—whether it's Google or Amazon or Microsoft. We pay our service providers for these wires and links to the IP addresses. The cables turn into data transfer cables due to routers and modems. Routers wirelessly transfer data to a device, then the device sends it back to the router, which sends it back to the modem, which then sends it through the wires to the necessary location. If multiple people are attached to the router, it will use the specific IP address to identify which files and requests need to go where. When a file is sent from one place to another through these wires, it's broken down into small pieces with instructions on how to recreate the file once it's received. This back-and-forth transfer of data and information makes up the internet.

2   How does your body know when to burp?

A burp is gas in the stomach that escapes up the esophagus. When there is too much gas in the stomach, the gas can escape, and a burp happens.

3   How do you recycle old paper to use it again?

Tear up newspaper or scrap paper and add hot water. Beat the paper and water in a blender and mix in starch. Pour the pulp into a flat pan. Slide a screen into the bottom of the pan and spread it out so that the pulp is covered evenly. Lift the screen out of the pan carefully and let it drain for a minute. Put the screen pulp-side up on a blotter on top of a newspaper. Roll a rolling pin over the sandwich of blotter paper to squeeze out the water. Take off the top newspaper and flip the blotter and the screen carefully, then let it dry for 12–24 hours.

4   How does a vacuum work?

When the start switch is activated, it sends volts to the motor, which drives the suction fan. When the motor is running, air let in behind the fan creates the suction needed. The air carries dust and debris through the fan into a capsule, and the extra air exits via the exhaust port.

5   How does your body digest new food?

The mouth is the gateway to the digestive system. The mouth breaks down food and adds saliva. Saliva contains enzymes that start breaking down food immediately. The food is then swallowed through the esophagus, which is a tube that runs from your mouth to your stomach. Gastric juices (a mix of acid and enzymes) in the stomach break down the food you eat, turning it into liquid. The food then moves into the small intestine. The first part of the small intestine is the duodenum, where more digestive juices are found such as bile. Bile is made in the liver and stored in the gallbladder. Bile and enzymes from the pancreas break down the proteins, fats, and carbohydrates, and it's here that the body absorbs the vitamins and minerals from the food. The remainder then moves to the large intestine, where it absorbs water and salt. The body then releases the remaining waste it does not need.

CONCLUSION

To become better at coming up with creative and innovative ideas, it's important to understand what's actually happening, and this means you need to ask the big questions: what, who, where, and when. You also need to ask how, and as you saw, "how" questions often lead to more information about processes and situations. The more you understand processes, the more ideas you will have about how to improve them. Keep asking these big five questions regularly, and soon it will become a natural part of your thinking.

CHAPTER 4

W H Y ?

You may have noticed in the last chapter that one of the big questions wasn't included—the question "why?" And why is that? **"Why"** is so important that it deserves an entire chapter. Asking why will give you a reason or purpose behind an action. This is critically important in idea generation.

You should actively be using "why" to question everything. Yes, everything! We naturally take so many actions without thinking, and it's important to ask ourselves *why* we're doing that. Why did you decide to do what you did? Why are other people doing what they do? When you begin questioning everything with why, you'll understand the root causes of actions and problems, which will help you come up with relevant ideas.

Let's say Ariel decides to go to a coffee shop to do work. I notice this and begin to ask questions:

1 **What** is she doing?

   She's going to work at a coffee shop.

2 **Who** is she doing this with?

   She's by herself but is interacting with the baristas.

3 **When?**

   It's currently 8:15 p.m.

4 **Where** is she doing this?

   At a local coffee shop downtown.

5 **How** is she doing this?

   She seems to have all of her work materials and technology with her. It looks like she walked to the coffee shop and is now connecting to the Wi-Fi in the shop to work on her laptop.

6 **Why** is she doing this?

   This is where it gets tricky. We don't know why she might be doing this, but it could be for a lot of reasons. Maybe she has a meeting there? Maybe her Wi-Fi doesn't work at home? Maybe she's on a business trip and is working remotely? Maybe she's not working at all and is just there to write a book in her free time?

Notice how "why" questions can lead to more information and potential problems. Also, you can't always answer "why" questions by just observing. We can't know for sure why Ariel went to the coffee shop without asking her. With "why" questions, it's important to ask people for the answers.

But you also need to be aware of something called a "false why." If someone has an answer to a "why" question, but their answer isn't accurate, then it's a false why. If you're in the workplace and you ask why we do a certain process in a certain way, keep in mind that one person may believe the reason why is different from another person's answer. So, it's okay to ask the question to multiple people, because you need to gain an understanding and find the true answers. Why can be a tricky question, and it requires a deep understanding to answer accurately.

EXERCISE 9:
QUESTION EVERYTHING

Instructions: Are you ready? It's time to question everything. This task may look similar to some of the previous exercises, but it's not. In this exercise, write down:

- Three "why" questions about life in general.
- Three "why" questions about yourself and your actions, reasons, and motives.
- Three "why" questions about your friends and their actions, reasons, and motives.
- Three "why" questions about random people you see in public and their actions, reasons, and motives.
- Three "why" questions about family and your family members' actions, reasons, and motives.
- Three "why" questions about work and the reasons and motives behind how things are done there.
- Two "why" questions about whatever you want.

Once you're done, instead of looking up the answers, I want you to start conversations. Speak with a friend, and ask them to answer your "why" questions. Speak to a stranger, and ask them about your "why" questions. Talk to your family about the "why" questions related to them. Finally, speak to someone at work about the three "why" questions relating to your coworkers, bosses, or job. Take notes about these conversations. Don't be shy. In order to fully complete this exercise, you must ask all of the people directly about the "why" questions that relate to them. When you do this, ask honestly and kindly, and make sure not to rub the person the wrong way. Asking random questions can feel intimidating, but sincere curiosity can be infectious, and people may appreciate the chance to open up about their motivations or share some of their knowledge.

Add notes on these conversations in your notebook.

Life:

1 _____

2 _____

3 _____

Yourself:

1 _____

2 _____

3 _____

Friends:

1 _____

2 _____

3 _____

About a stranger:

1 _____

2 _____

3 _____

Family:

1 _____

2 _____

3 _____

Work:

1 _____

2 _____

3 _____

Your choice:

1 _____

2 _____

While you might regularly ask "why" questions to the people you know, it's even more important to ask a stranger. Strangers help you step out of your comfort zone and give you different perspectives than friends, family, and coworkers who share similar views or interests with you. I recommend actively talking to strangers to understand how people may see questions, problems, or ideas differently.

CONCLUSION

Asking why is extremely important. It's a base question to gain an understanding about your own and other people's reasons and purpose. Discussing these whys with other people, especially strangers, can be extremely beneficial because it can lead to different views and even different ways of thinking about the questions.

CHAPTER 5

THE WHY
3X RULE

So, you've gotten into the habit of asking more questions and asking why. But sometimes, the answer you receive doesn't seem to reach the root cause of the issue—that is, the real problem at the heart of the matter. The next step is taking yourself through what I call the "Why 3x Rule." This powerful rule helps you find and understand the root causes of an issue more effectively. It also enables you to come up with ideas you can apply to make a real difference—game-changing ideas.

Start with a problem, need, want, or statement. Then ask, "Why is that a problem, need, or want?" or "Why is that happening?" Answering this question will give you a conclusion. Take this conclusion, and ask why again. This allows you to dig even deeper. Then take the second conclusion, and ask why again. This will dig into the root cause of an issue. Remember when you were a kid and you used to ask, "why?" And when your parents answered, you'd ask, "but why?" and so on. It's just like that.

Let's see how this works in practice. Say you own a specialty convenience store, and you notice that spice sales have gone down. That is a problem. First, you ask, "Why have my spice sales gone down?" Maybe the answer is because customers have been buying fewer spices. That would make sense. Now, if you were to stop here, you could say, "Oh, let's just advertise spices more!" However, that could be a misdiagnosis or a false why.

Ask again, "Why are customers buying fewer spices?" After some research, you find out that customers don't feel comfortable buying spices they have never heard of or don't know anything about. You could stop here again and say, "Ah, well we just need to stock different spices." However, you may still be jumping to conclusions.

You know you've provided new spices that have sold before, so you ask again, "Why are customers not willing to buy new spices now when they were willing to before?" You then learn that a former employee at the store, Jeff, was an expert in spices and used to educate customers and help them decide what to purchase, but he left a month ago.

This gets you to the root of the problem: customers are not being educated about new spice options in the store. You need a spice expert on hand to help you sell more spices. Notice how hiring a new employee is a very different conclusion than advertising spices more. You would have never arrived at the true conclusion had you not followed the Why 3x Rule.

Not fully understanding the root cause of a problem happens regularly because people don't keep questioning their early conclusions. You may think you know the answer to why something is happening, since it seems to be apparent, but if you keep digging, you can often find different reasons why people do the things they do or why something is occurring. Say your new employees consistently respond in staff surveys that they aren't extremely satisfied with their job. You ask, "Why aren't you satisfied with your job?" Their response is that they feel the job they have and the job they were promised don't line up. Your conclusion is that the job requirements are badly written and need to be adjusted.

You ask why again. "Why do the job they were promised and their actual job not line up?" The human resource teams and the work teams don't seem be on the same page about the job requirements. The conclusion you might come to is, "Great, if we just have the teams more effectively communicate, then the problem is solved." Or is it?

Ask again, "Why are the teams not on the same page?" After asking around, you find that the teams feel their leaders are unclear about the job requirements in the first place. Unclear leadership is a larger issue than a slight misunderstanding, but you wouldn't have known this if you hadn't dug down to the root of the problem.

EXERCISE 10:
THE WHY 3X RULE
IN PRACTICE

Instructions: Congratulations! You've made it this far into the book, and you're still going. Let's put your motives to the test with the Why 3x Rule. I want you to answer the question: "Why have you kept reading up to this point?" For each answer, you need to dig down and ask Why 3x to find out your true motives for reading.

Fill out the answers for the first three whys. The second set of whys is for your own personal questions (either business or personal). Fill those out too. The more practice you have, the more you will be able to apply the rule!

Why are you still reading this book?

Why answer one:

_____

_____

_____

Ask why about the previous answer.

Why answer two:

_____

_____

_____

Ask why about the previous answer one more time.

Why answer three:

_____

_____

_____

_____

Your question:

_____

Why answer one:

_____

_____

_____

Ask why about the previous answer.

Why answer two:

_____

_____

_____

Ask why about the previous answer one more time.

Why answer three:

_____

_____

_____

CONCLUSION

If you want to make a real difference, you need to stop looking at the symptoms and start looking for the root cause of them. If you're a doctor, you don't want to diagnose based on the symptoms alone—you want to examine and conduct tests on the patient in order to diagnose the underlying problem. Life works in the same way. An idea that treats a symptom might be mildly successful, but if your idea helps to cure a real problem, then you know you're making a true impact. It's critical to use the Why 3x Rule in everyday life because it's easy to naturally jump to conclusions. However, if you're diligent, you can find the real issues and tackle them to make a huge difference.

CHAPTER 6

WHAT INSPIRED THAT?

Do you ever look at something and think, "I wonder how they thought of that?" Often, we stop to think about it for a second, then just let the thought go. This time, I'm going to challenge you to think more deeply. If you're having trouble identifying problems, needs, and wants, then this chapter will be especially helpful. We'll take the process from the previous chapters and look at how it works in reverse to find problems, needs, wants, and questions.

WHY DOES THIS EXIST?

Everything was created for a reason, but not all reasons are obvious. We often take many things, events, and items for granted, without ever asking why they were created in the first place. Some objects are easier to decipher than others. For example, why was an umbrella created? Someone wanted to stay dry when it was raining. (Feel free to also use the Why 3x Rule here to dig deeper into the meaning of objects or processes.) Some objects have multiple reasons for their creation. For example, why was a smartphone created? Well, we needed a way to make phone calls without being attached to a landline. We wanted access to the internet at all times. We wanted the ability to send messages to friends, and so on.

HOW DOES THIS HELP?

So far, we have trained your brain to identify questions, problems, needs, and wants, but sometimes that's easier said than done. As such, it can be helpful to look at things that already exist. Looking at objects or processes and identifying why they were created helps you come up with more ideas in your everyday environment. It provides the following benefits:

- It gives you a different method of idea creation—one that might be more helpful to you than starting from the perspective of finding problems, wants, or needs.

- It inspires you to see problems, needs, wants, or questions that you hadn't noticed before in your everyday environment.

- It helps you realize new problems that might exist in current items or processes but that haven't been addressed or identified yet.

- By working backward, you'll see how people moved from problem to idea, and this will help you develop solutions and ideas for the problems you come up with.

Looking at why items or processes were created means you can look at problems differently. Instead of looking for problems that people are currently facing, you're looking at problems that people faced in the past and the solutions they came up with to resolve them. These solutions and ideas are also elite, as they have survived in the market for a long time, and people still use these items or processes every day. You're looking at ideas that you know work, which can be inspiring when it comes to creating your own ideas.

However, just because an item has existed for a long time doesn't mean there aren't new problems and solutions that can improve that item. Looking at why an item exists may reveal problems not yet dealt with. Take a look at a backpack and try to figure out why it was created. The answer may be: it helps you carry more than you can hold in your hands, and it has compartments so you can organize your belongings. You may also discover that you use a backpack to keep your belongings safe. But if you stop to ask, "Is this really the best way to keep my belongings safe?" this reveals a problem.

You don't feel that items in a backpack are particularly safe, yet you want a safe way to carry your belongings on your back. Notice how digging into the reason why items were created can sometimes lead to new problems, needs, wants, and questions? This, in turn, leads to more ideas. In section 3, we'll go through the process of creating ideas by starting with problems. In this case, one example of a solution or idea could be: backpacks should have locks. For now, it's important to consider each item and take a deep look at it.

The backpack example also shows you how people have gone from problem to solution, and what solutions to problems look like. A backpack is one way of solving the problem of "how to carry a lot of heavy things" or "how to carry more than I can hold in my hands." You can think through the development process behind how backpacks came to be. This continual evaluation of identifying the problem and solution—and mapping how people moved from the problem to their idea—will train your brain to do this with problems you identify. This is an extremely useful skill to have when seeking to turn problems into meaningful ideas.

EXERCISE 11:
WHAT INSPIRED THAT?

Instructions: Now you'll find a list of items, processes, and events. Make some notes about why you think they were created, what problems they solve or solved in the past, and what purpose they have. Use the Why 3x Rule if you get stuck.

- Suits
- Tea
- Licenses
- Elementary/primary school
- Self-checkouts
- Marathons
- Job training
- Journalism
- The Olympics
- Virtual bank accounts

Next you'll find three examples. For each of the ten items, there are many reasons why the item was created, many problems it may solve, and many purposes it continues to serve. These example answers are by no means the only answers. The answers below are meant to be a guide to how to go about the exercise, to jump-start your own thinking about the other topics.

Elementary/Primary School

Why it was created:

- Elementary and primary schools allow children to get more out of education and save parents time. The information is taught by people specialized in the teaching field, who can communicate information more effectively for young students.

What problem it solves/solved:

- Parents do not have enough time to teach children to the quality standards they desire.
- Parents may not be the best communicators or may not have the expertise to teach children at a high level.

What purpose it continues to provide:

- Today, a formalized education system for children continues to provide a standardized way that we can give information to individuals to help them learn. It still saves parents time and allows children to get more out of their education.

Self-Checkouts

Why it was created:

- Self-checkouts provide an easy, efficient way to make purchases, saving both customers and store employees time, as well as saving stores money and space.

What problem it solves/solved:

- Checking out takes a long time for customers.
- Having a lot of employees working on the checkout is expensive.

- Having a full checkout line takes away potential space that could be used for other items.

What purpose it continues to provide:

- Today, self-checkouts continue to save customers and stores time and space. They also save stores money because they hire fewer employees. Self-checkout systems now integrate with stores' inventory in inventory management systems. They can help a store know when to order more of each product and what products customers are buying.

The Olympics

Why it was created:

- The Olympic Games were created to identify and determine which country has the best athletes. It also serves as entertainment for non-athletes.

What problem it solves/solved:

- There were no universal rules for sports.
- There was no way of organizing and objectively identifying the best athletes in the world.
- There was no organization that allowed many countries to compete at events at once.

What purpose it continues to provide:

- Today, the Olympics not only provides entertainment and a universal playing field for all countries, but the games offer a universal stage for countries and athletes to share messages about things they are passionate about.

CONCLUSION

This simple trick of studying why items or processes were created can often inspire new ideas, problems, needs, and wants for you. Infinite objects and events surround you. Practice this strategy and use it often. After some practice, you'll actively feel the inspiration that these past innovators felt when creating their ideas. Having this many inspiring things to think about will almost feel like cheating, since it will help you come up with many more ideas. This same drill can be applied to systems, objects, processes, actions, and events—both in the workplace and in everyday life.

We have come to a rare moment. Here, **you** get to determine what comes next. Everyone's brains work differently, so the chapter you read next should be determined by how confident you're feeling in your skills, based on the sections you've read so far. Do you believe you can effectively come up with problems, needs, wants, and questions? Can you follow the Why 3x Rule and find inspiration from existing items? If so, then I suggest you read the next chapter, which shows you what to do once you have identified these problems, needs, wants, and questions.

If you're still having trouble, that's okay. I suggest you read chapter 26 next. Chapter 26 is about "hacking" your own brain to increase the number of ideas you can come up with. This chapter should kick-start your thinking to help you find more problems, needs, and wants in your everyday life. The choice is yours.

SECTION 2

//

ERASING
STIGMAS

Fair warning: This next section can be the most difficult part of the process to master. You're going to take everything you perceive as normal and challenge it. So, get ready to twist your brain as you uproot the building blocks you currently use to solve problems!

CHAPTER 7

DEFINING
A STIGMA

B y this point, you've used the techniques we've covered so far to identify many problems, needs, and wants. Your mind has probably already leaped to come up with solutions to those problems. It's natural to want to solve problems immediately, but before you write down the solutions, it's important to identify, confront, and erase your stigmas first so that you can come up with the best ideas. In this chapter, we'll look at how to identify your own stigmas and those around you.

Most people underestimate how crucial finding and erasing stigmas is. It's the most important step in creative problem-solving, because you need to come up with all of the possible solutions—not just the obvious ones or those based on assumptions. If you truly want the most game-changing ideas, it's vital that you identify and erase stigmas. In doing so, you'll create guidelines for your solutions to follow.

HOW DO STIGMAS AFFECT US?

Pause for a second and imagine yourself in the following situation. You are sitting in a lecture next to your boss and many strangers. 500 people in the audience sit at tables listening to a speaker on a slightly elevated stage. The speaker pauses during her speech. She pulls out a $100 bill. She says to the audience, "The first audience member on stage can have $100." Do you run up on stage? Take a second to play this out in your head before answering.

If you're even a little hesitant to say yes, then you're not alone. I've seen this happen in speeches before, and sometimes it takes more than a full minute for someone to get the courage to go up on stage. But why? Everyone wants free money, especially if you can get $100 for little to no work. Why would you *not* want to claim that? What's stopping you?

What's stopping you is a stigma. **Stigmas** are rules or guidelines that we feel the need to follow, even though they may not apply to our present situation or may not be true at all. Stigmas are everywhere. Let's take a closer look at the $100-bill scenario. What are some stigmas that stop people from going on stage when the presenter is giving away free money?

- We believe that people don't just give out free money. Therefore, the situation is too good to be true.
- We believe that when a speaker is giving a presentation, the stage is only for the speaker and event staff.
- We believe that in a business setting, we shouldn't do anything erratic or unprofessional.
- We're taught to sit in our seats and be quiet during a presentation to show respect.

Those are just a few stigmas, but many more come into play and stop us from going to claim that free money.

WHERE DO STIGMAS COME FROM?

If you stop to think about it, you'll notice many stigmas, but where do they come from? An individual may have many stigmas developed by:

- **Society's standards**
- **The way they were raised**
- **Habits they've formed**
- **Repeated actions:** Doing the same thing over and over again.
- **A lack of visible change:** There has not been a change in the way things have been done for a long time.
- **Social influence:** Top companies or people are doing it one way.
- **Acceptance:** People on the receiving end have come to accept that things are done in one way, for example, in business cases, the customers tend to display the same behavior over time.
- **How a set of information is phrased, viewed, or presented**

We operate in our daily lives by following two sets of rules: laws and society's standards. Laws are the set of rules written by our government. Breaking them results in punishment. Obviously, breaking the law is a bad idea. On the other hand, it's not necessarily bad if society's standards are broken. Society's standards are based on assumptions that people make about a situation. The assumption follows the way the majority of people in that society act, but acting in a different way doesn't necessarily bring negative consequences.

Society's standards are sometimes the hardest stigmas to identify, but breaking one may lead to an increase in efficiency or knowledge. One common social stigma assumes that we shouldn't discuss religion or politics at the dinner table. While this may be important in keeping friendships, some situations call for breaking this stigma. It's important to understand opposing viewpoints and political issues—and talking with friends or peers can be a great way to increase our knowledge here. If we don't seek a full view, we may make uneducated decisions.

The second type of stigma is based on how people are raised. Since everyone was raised differently, not everyone shares a uniform set of stigmas. These stigmas are developed based on the values you grew up with. Say you were raised to believe you should always bring a gift to a person's house when you visit them. If someone shows up to your house without a gift, you think this is rude. However, that person may not have been raised with this same value, so they have no idea that you feel it's rude. This stigma is a result of assumptions that aren't shared. The visitor likely doesn't intend to be rude, but they don't share your assumption that a gift is necessary.

Another type of stigma arises from doing things "the way they've always been done" or "the way things are." This is also known as the *status quo.* The status quo exists in the wider world, in individual societies, and in businesses. These stigmas can be powerful, and especially in business situations, finding and erasing them is hugely important, since they often prevent businesses from moving forward with the times, staying relevant, and improving their offerings. We'll look at how to challenge the status quo in more depth in chapter 12.

The next set of stigmas results from social influence. We see powerful, famous people and companies doing things one way, so we assume we must also do things that same way. This is a common stigma, but it's usually easy to catch when you stop to notice that not *everyone* does it. For example, if your favorite fitness model only eats carbs at very specific times of day, you may also make that an internal rule. However, you can observe that everyone else still eats carbs whenever they want. These stigmas are not common to all of society and only apply to some people, which makes them easy to identify.

The next type of stigma is based on acceptance. If the people you interact with—or in a business case, the customers—have been accepting the same thing in the same way for a long time, then they likely expect that you won't change that offering. These people or customers may be important to you, but you still need to test out new ideas. In fact, the person or customer may like the new idea even better than the old one they'd previously been happy to accept. It's always important to keep other people and your customers in mind, but it's just as important to challenge the way things are done to make sure there's not a better possible way.

For example, say Business A offers balloons. They have been selling balloons for more than 20 years, and they are a top balloon-selling company. Customers have been accepting these balloons for decades. Because of this repeated acceptance, Business A may miss or not be aware of potential improvements such as helium-filled balloons, which last longer.

This also applies to your personal life. Say Jerry and Marge are best friends. For the past year, Jerry has agreed to make Marge dinner every Saturday. At the start, Marge requested that Jerry make steak, so he does. Since Marge is always okay with steak, Jerry assumes that's what she still wants, so Jerry no longer thinks about other options. On Saturdays, he's so used to making steak and Marge eating it that he's decided—consciously or not—that this is the only option. On the contrary, Marge might like something different now or Jerry might have another specialty that Marge hasn't tried yet.

We also internalize a number of information stigmas. These stigmas are based on the ways that information is delivered or received. This is the most important and dangerous type of stigma. Consider the Vietnam War, which is part of both the American and Vietnamese school curriculums. The information taught in each country's respective school system is drastically different. Information and problems can be skewed, forcing you to look at things one way when maybe you should be looking at them in another way.

We're exposed to this kind of skewed information daily, with advertisements about the "best products" or commercials with graphs displaying information intended to make us believe one thing is true. Words and pictures are incredibly powerful, and it's important to dig deeper into everything you hear. Once you're able to identify information stigmas, you can begin erasing these stigmas.

Lastly, we form stigmas based on habits. These are stigmas you've created yourself, based on the way you've done things in the past. It's almost like the flip side of the acceptance stigma. Maybe you're the person buying the same balloons for years without noticing that the helium-filled kind offered by the other shop is a much better deal. Or let's say you take a shower daily and have done so for the past 20 years. If someone told you they haven't showered in three days, that might gross you out. However, lots of studies report that it's healthier if we shower about twice a week. So, your reaction to your friend's less rigorous bathing schedule is a stigma created by a habit. Identifying habits is often a great way to start finding stigmas, as they're things you commonly do but often don't even notice you're doing.

EXERCISE 12:

FINDING HABITS

Instructions: Examine your life and look for your own habits. Find 10 and write them down. Then ask yourself why you have that habit. If your answer is, "Because I've always done it that way," then circle that habit and question it further.

Habit:

_____

Why:

_____

Habit:

_____

Why:

_____

Habit:

_____

Why:

_____

Habit:

_____

Why:

_____

Habit:

_____

Why:

_____

Habit:

_____

Why:

_____

Habit:

_____

Why:

_____

Habit:

_____

Why:

_____

Habit: _____

Why: _____

Habit: _____

Why: _____

WHY DO WE HAVE STIGMAS?

Since we've seen that stigmas can be dangerous, the obvious question is why do we have them? The answer is because our brains can only handle so many problems and so much information at once. Stigmas help people avoid trivial problems, save time, and improve efficiency. For example, you don't want to think about whether you should put on your jeans with your left foot or your right foot every day.

Sometimes, the answer to a problem can become much simpler if you identify the necessary rules or stigmas that *don't* apply. For example, if you drive the same car to work every day and it breaks down one day, you may think, "I need to take a day off work to go and get the car fixed to drive to work!" This is because you have stigmas and habits about driving to work. However, a much simpler answer would be just to get a taxi to work and wait to fix it over the weekend. In more complex problems, not identifying and erasing stigmas can often stop you from seeing a simple solution. Say a company is looking to hire a new person for a very specific skill set. Often, they'll go straight to the market and look for new people, because they haven't identified their stigmas. For example, have they looked around in their own company? Maybe someone in their workforce already has the skills and talent they're looking for and could move into the position.

In chapter 10, we'll expand on this and provide strategies to help you identify your stigmas before solving problems, needs, and wants.

EXERCISE 13:
SPOTTING STIGMAS

Instructions: In this exercise, try to think of an example of a stigma you have. If you can't, refer to the example for a directed prompt.

Example: Come up with a stigma you might have if you were tasked with building a playground. Sometimes, it's easier to identify stigmas if you narrow your thinking down to a specific topic.

_____

_____

_____

CONCLUSION

It's important to start identifying and challenging the stigmas you may have, so you can begin to identify all of the possible ideas. In the playground example, you may think you need slides and swings because most playgrounds have them, but in order for a playground to work, you just need to create space where people can play. Therefore, the assumption that specific equipment is necessary is a stigma. Instead, you could paint on the concrete and create four-square and hopscotch or add small goals to either end of a grassy field for a soccer game. Finding an answer to a problem can become much simpler if you identify the rules or stigmas that are limiting your options. This can lead to more effective brainstorming because it will help you to identify which guidelines apply to your current situation. Finding stigmas can be challenging, but don't be discouraged. Focus on the strategies in this chapter in your everyday life and you'll soon spot your stigmas!

CHAPTER 8

FINDING AND ERASING STIGMAS IN PRACTICE

S tigmas are often hard to find because you're trained to make assumptions, but when it comes to making creative solutions, it's imperative that you consider all of the possible options. This chapter is all about getting some practice, so we'll focus on lots of exercises to practice finding, evaluating, and erasing stigmas. Let's get started with some brain exercises.

EXERCISE 14:
YOUR MASTERPIECE

Instructions: Now it's time to release your creativity. There are parts of pictures here—finish them however you imagine it makes sense. (If it is easier for you, feel free to trace them or approximately draw the scribble in your notebook and work from there.)

1

2

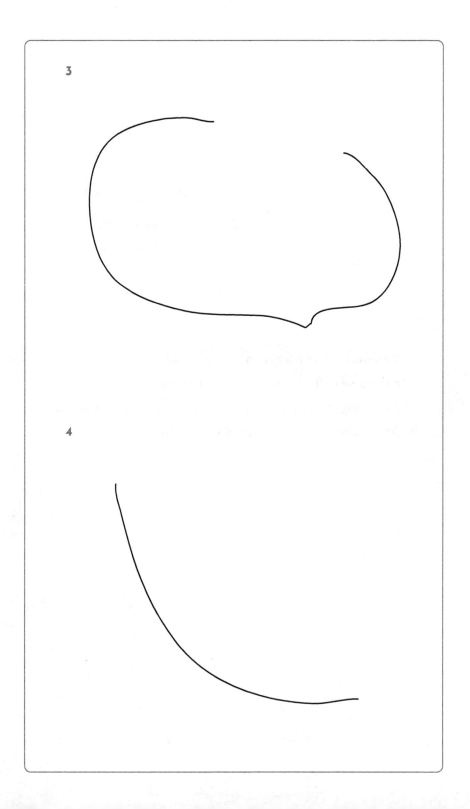

3

4

5

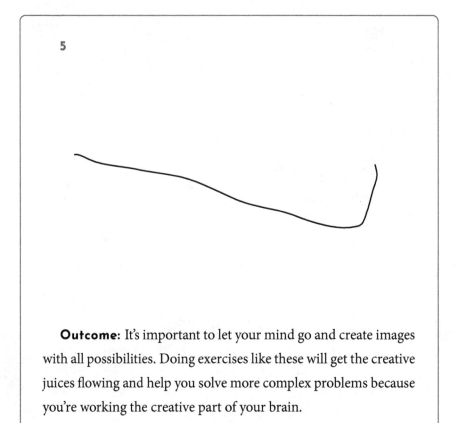

Outcome: It's important to let your mind go and create images with all possibilities. Doing exercises like these will get the creative juices flowing and help you solve more complex problems because you're working the creative part of your brain.

EXERCISE 15:
CURRENT STIGMAS
ABOUT A PROBLEM

Instructions: Take a problem you're facing in life, your job, or business. Write down some stigmas you're facing in that problem. Then think of three potential new solutions that break the stigmas you've identified.

Stigmas

1 _____

2 _____

3 _____

New Solutions

1 _____

2 _____

3 _____

Outcome: It's important to start practicing the habit of looking at all possibilities. The more possibilities you leave open, the more you'll be able to see solutions that you don't normally see.

EXERCISE 16:
THE FOX, THE CHICKEN, AND THE CORN

Instructions: Consider the following example. A woman has to move a fox, a chicken, and a bag of corn across a river. She has one rowboat that can only hold either her and the fox, her and the bag of corn, or her and the chicken. She must get the chicken, fox, and corn across safely, but there is a problem. If the fox is left alone with the chicken, the fox will eat the chicken. If the chicken is left alone with the corn, the chicken will eat the corn. How does the woman do it?

Outcome: It might help to draw the answer or problem out step by step in an options tree. The first move is for the woman to take the chicken across the river. If she doesn't, then either the corn or the chicken will be compromised. Once the chicken is on the other side of the river, she goes back and can either take the fox or the corn. Let's say she takes the corn across the river next and drops it off. However, the chicken and the corn can't be left alone—otherwise, the corn will be eaten. So she takes the chicken back across the river, so it's not alone with the corn, and leaves the corn. When she gets to the other side, she leaves the chicken on the original side. Since the fox and chicken can't be left alone, she takes the fox across the river. The fox and the corn can be left together, so she drops off the fox, then she goes back one more time to get the chicken.

Why is this problem so hard? Well, we have a stigma that the woman must cross the river and can take only one thing with her, but we didn't include the possibility that she can bring something back on the boat. This is a stigma we may have naturally created while trying to solve the problem. It's important to list your stigmas before considering the problems to avoid becoming stuck without providing a quality solution.

START

The woman takes the chicken across the river.

Then, she takes across the bag of corn.

She brings the chicken with her on the way back.

She takes the fox across, leaving the chicken behind.

She then returns for the chicken.

Finally, she takes the chicken across.

FINISH

EXERCISE 17:
THE BOX PROBLEM

Instructions: Using four straight lines (no curves!) or fewer, connect all nine dots to each other without taking your pencil off the page. If you figure it out with four lines, try it again with three lines, two lines, or even one line!

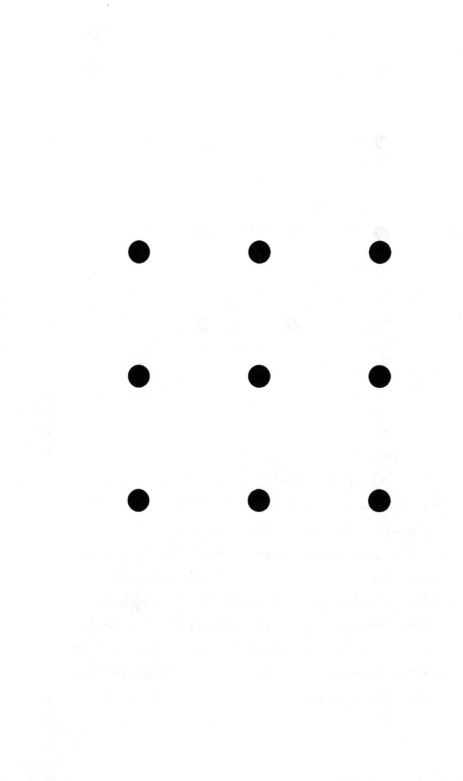

Outcome: Here, you can see the answer to the box problem:

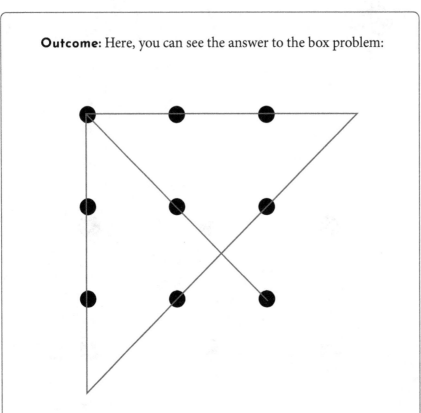

This is a great problem to help you evaluate your stigmas. Did you try only drawing lines inside the box? This is actually where the expression "think outside the box" came from. It's important not to make assumptions before you even evaluate the problem. Here, many people assume you have to draw lines that only extend within the box's corners. Did you have trouble completing the exercise using three, two, or one line(s)? Did you consider bending the paper, or ripping it out of the book, or even drawing one big fat line? There are no set rules, but the assumption of rules can hinder you from finding a solution.

EXERCISE 18:
THE TRICKY EQUATION

Instructions: Can you make this equation true by adding just one line? (Hint: There are two answers.)

$$1 + 5 + 5 = 150$$

Outcome: The answer is to add a line to the + sign or the = sign. Were you caught by the stigma of only changing the numbers? Did you not think about the + sign? Did you end up getting both solutions? In the two solutions, we add a line to turn the + sign into a number 4 (making 145), and we change the = sign into a does not equal sign (≠).

$$1\,4\,5 + 5 = 150$$

$$1 + 5 + 5 \neq 150$$

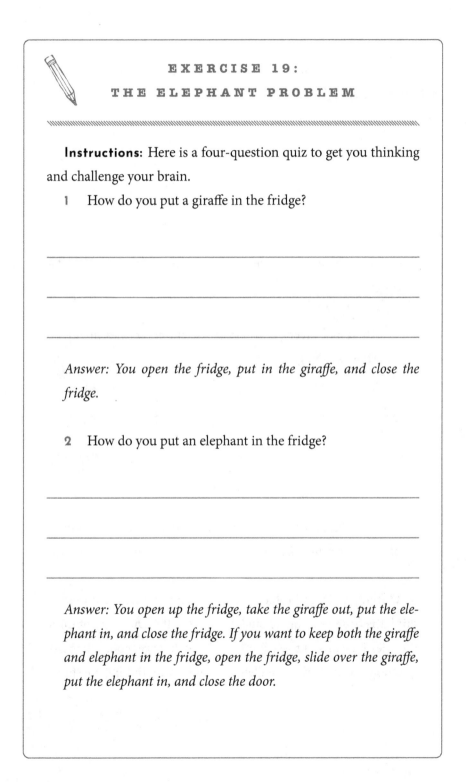

EXERCISE 19:
THE ELEPHANT PROBLEM

Instructions: Here is a four-question quiz to get you thinking and challenge your brain.

1   How do you put a giraffe in the fridge?

_____

_____

_____

Answer: You open the fridge, put in the giraffe, and close the fridge.

2   How do you put an elephant in the fridge?

_____

_____

_____

Answer: You open up the fridge, take the giraffe out, put the elephant in, and close the fridge. If you want to keep both the giraffe and elephant in the fridge, open the fridge, slide over the giraffe, put the elephant in, and close the door.

3   The lion is hosting an animal conference. All the animals except a few attend. Who doesn't attend?

_____

_____

_____

Answer: The elephant and/or the giraffe! They are still in the fridge.

4   There is a river you must cross, but crocodiles inhabit it. How do you get across?

_____

_____

_____

Answer: There are lots of ways to get across, but the easiest is probably just to swim. The crocodiles are all at the animal conference!

Outcome: These problems involve many stigmas. Did you not think the fridge was big enough for the giraffe? Did you not think the questions linked to each other? Did you forget about the prior questions? This exercise challenges stigmas with linking questions.

EXERCISE 20:
GLASSES OF ORANGE JUICE

Instructions: There are six glasses of orange juice spaced on a table. By moving only one cup, can you make it so that only alternating cups have orange juice in them?

Outcome: Did you consider pouring one glass of orange juice into another glass? Or did you only consider rearranging the glasses themselves to find a way to alternate the full cups with the empty ones? This is another common problem where people get lost in stigmas.

CONCLUSION

As you may have found in these practice problems, finding, evaluating, and erasing stigmas can be complicated and challenging. If you're interested in more problems like these, you can look up lateral thinking problems, brain teasers, creativity challenges, or "think outside the box" problems.

Finding, evaluating, and erasing stigmas is not easy. But it's important to stay patient with finding stigmas and make sure you exercise all of your options. Working with a team and getting other points of view can also help dramatically.

CHAPTER 9

ERASING

STIGMAS

THROUGH PLAY

N ow that you've warmed your brain up and started finding and erasing stigmas, you can take it a step further by
engaging in play. You might think that play is something
for children, and it's true that children are typically experts in play.
They create and make games, and their brains are constantly buzzing
with opportunities. As a result, they sometimes see creative solutions
where adults are blinded by stigmas. When identifying stigmas and
becoming more creative, being an expert in play can be extremely
helpful. Play isn't just for kids, as you'll see in this chapter.

EXERCISE 21:
THE PARKING LOT PROBLEM

Instructions: In a well-known experiment, first graders in Hong Kong were given 20 seconds to solve the following problem. Most of them did, but it takes some adults up to an hour to solve. Give it a go.

What space number is the car parked in?

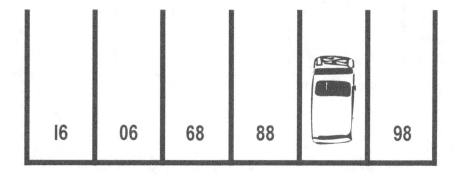

Outcome: Give up? Or did you get it? The answer is 87. The reason is that we're looking at the spots upside down! Consider the picture flipped.

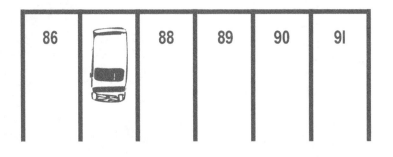

Much easier to see, right? But why are first graders able to solve this in 20 seconds while it takes adults minutes or even hours? This is a perfect example of stigmas. The information is given in a way where we see numbers: 16, 06, 68, 88, and 98. Those numbers are all clear and can be read in one direction. Because that's the way the information is presented, we *assume* that the picture is oriented correctly, but in fact, it's the opposite.

The fact that children can solve this problem demonstrates their ability to make fewer assumptions and apply fewer stigmas when solving the problem. But why are they so creative and able to solve problems so quickly compared to adults? As we get older, we take in more information about the world. Our brain makes assumptions based on that information. Since children have accumulated less information, they make fewer assumptions. They are more open to all of the possibilities, and therefore they are more creative in their solutions. Children have a powerful sense of creativity that adults sometimes struggle to find.

HOW DOES PLAY HELP?

You can begin to reverse this process of losing your creativity by engaging in play. Consistently playing will help you train your brain to go back to its more primal instincts, where there are no rules and anything can happen. When looking to identify stigmas, being an expert in play can be extremely helpful. Play will not only help you find more stigmas but will also help you ask more deep and challenging questions. It will drive you to become exponentially more creative overall. This is because play takes you out of your normal, everyday state. It puts your brain in a new mindset—and that difference in thinking drives creativity.

According to Helpguide.org, play in adults can relieve stress, improve brain function, stimulate and boost creativity, improve relationships and connections, keep you feeling energetic, encourage cooperation, develop social skills, and heal emotional wounds. So don't be embarrassed by play—in fact, it may be exactly what you need!

Have you ever found yourself checking your work email or doing a task while a member of your family asks you to come and play? Maybe your friends want you to go and play a game, but you're just too busy? It's time to stop being too busy and play much more.

EXERCISE 22:
COLOR OUTSIDE THE LINES

Instructions: I'm going to provide you with a picture and give you two rules:

1   You must color outside the lines. Lines are not your boundaries.

2   Each section must have multiple colors involved.

Go and have fun! (If it is easier for you, feel free to trace or roughly draw this image.)

Outcome: It's important to get rid of stigmas such as coloring inside the lines or using a color theme. Many people will default to coloring a frog green and only coloring in the lines, but there are many options to approach this exercise. For example, you can turn the image into a purple frog riding a pony, or you could make it a half-frog, half-snowman. Get your creative juices flowing, let your brain be free, and have fun!

HOW TO PLAY

Give yourself 15–20 minutes a day to let your mind be free and play. Whether it's creating a story in your head, playing with toys, getting moving, or creating a game, play is critical and can help you become more creative. One great way to improve your creativity is by engaging in free play. Free play means there are no rules—you make up the game and make up the adventure, and everything is a free-for-all.

If you're having trouble figuring out how to play, the National Institute of Play identifies seven types:

1 **Attunement play:** This is when two people are in tune with each other without specific confirmation of this. A simple example is when you stand on one side of a room and your friend stands on the other side. Smile at your friend. If they smile or laugh back, this is the base state of play.

2 **Body play and movement:** This is play based on your own physical movement—an exploration of body movements for pleasure.

A simple example of this is jumping as far as you can to test your body's limits or running around and playing a game.

3   **Object play:** This is play associated with curiosity around objects, where you use objects to play. A simple example of this is seeing how fast a spinning top can go around.

4   **Social play:** This is playing with others. A simple example of this is creating complex banter with a close friend.

5   **Imaginative and pretend play:** This is the ability to create your own sense of mind and engage in pretend play. It's key to innovation and creativity. A simple example is pretending to be a part of an imaginary reality.

6   **Storytelling-narrative play:** This is using and creating narratives to help foster fun experiences. A simple example of this is creating your own childhood storybook.

7   **Creative play:** This type of fantasy play takes the reality of our ordinary lives and turns it on its head to process and germinate new ideas—and shape and reshape those ideas. A simple example is creating a brand-new product using only things in the room.

As you can see, sometimes different types of play can overlap, and that's okay. There are lots of ways to play.

EXERCISE 23:

GO PLAY

Instructions: Stop what you're doing and put down the book. Don't worry—you can pick it up later, but it's time to take a break. Go and play! Do whatever you want. Let your mind go free.

CONCLUSION

Play is imperative in helping you return to a childlike state of being, where you're able to see past stigmas and come up with creative solutions. If you find yourself stuck on a problem, sometimes the best solution is to take a break and just go play! You should play regularly, daily even. Continuing to stretch your mind by playing will help you better identify stigmas and spark creative ideas.

CHAPTER 10

STIGMA
STRATEGIES

S o you've started to train your brain to identify and erase stigmas in everyday life, but what about when you have a specific problem? When you're trying to resolve a problem or create a solution and you're looking to identify the stigmas that might affect this, it's important to approach the problem with a sense of "zero knowledge." Take a look at the problem from square one—as if you've never seen a problem like this before. In this chapter, I'll show you four strategies to help you do this.

THE BLANK-PAPER APPROACH

One strategy is the blank-paper approach. When first solving a problem, take a blank piece of paper. Start listing the assumptions you have to identify what you think about the problem. You can write or even draw these assumptions if pictures make more sense to you. With each assumption, ask whether it's really necessary to the solution.

Before you write down an assumption, you need to be sure it's necessary. If you're doing this alone, either self-evaluate or ask a friend. If you're in a group and the vote is not unanimous, then the person or people who voted against it must explain their reasoning to the group. Then the assumption can be deleted or adjusted.

Say your business is creating a new children's water toy, something like a Super Soaker. One person says, "The toy must not be dangerous or hazardous." The group will obviously agree. The next person says, "The toy must be able to hold water." Well, not necessarily. Not all water toys actually hold water. Slip n' Slides don't, and plenty of other water toys don't either. So don't include this assumption when you try to think up a new water toy. Vetting assumptions to determine whether they're necessary conditions for a solution can improve the creativity of your solutions. Only write down the assumptions or rules that *absolutely* apply.

EXERCISE 24:
THE BLANK-PAPER APPROACH

Instructions: There are two options:

1   Using the blank-paper approach described previously, create a boat for two ladybugs that can sail 50 miles.

2   Using the blank-paper approach, imagine a way the shoe industry could make shoes more efficient or useful.

Outcome: Practicing the blank-paper approach for all types of problems can help you better identify stigmas. At this point, the actual working solution is less important than figuring out what we need to keep in mind and what assumptions we need to let go of as we work toward it. We'll work on the solution later, but for now, it's important now to just identify all the stigmas you have.

THE WILD-IMAGINATION STRATEGY

Another approach is the wild-imagination strategy. Basically, when approaching a problem, you create the wildest, most imaginative answers you can think of—either by yourself and/or with a team. You draw these out. You place the wild answers to your problems on a board. Then you slowly bring it back to reality by adding requirements. If you're doing this by yourself, then name one thing you can do to bring it back to reality, also known as a potential requirement. If you're doing this with a team, go around the room and everybody must name one requirement. The room then votes on whether that potential requirement is necessary to the problem. If it is, they edit the requirement. If they don't, they keep it and write it out as a stigma.

Here's an example in action. Let's say you want to create a plane for frogs. Everybody imagines their plane and draws it out, then they place theirs on the board. There are some wild inventions—some have wings, others have rockets, and a few have propellers. The first member of the group takes a look at the pictures and says, "The plane needs to be able to hold or carry a frog." The room agrees. This is a requirement, not a stigma. The next person says, "This is a plane—it shouldn't go to space." The room doesn't come to a 100 percent consensus on this. Why shouldn't it go to space? It might be faster. Therefore, it's a stigma, not a requirement. While the final answer may not be to take the plane into space, it's important not to eliminate it from the realm of possibilities.

EXERCISE 25:
THE WILD-IMAGINATION
STRATEGY

Instructions: Imagine a new way you can get to work more efficiently with a budget of $1,000 a day. Start with your wildest idea, then work it down to a reality. Make sure you write down the stigmas and requirements along the way.

Outcome: It can be extremely rewarding to practice finding stigmas attached to a real-life issue. Using this wild-imagination strategy can inspire new ideas that push the limits of what you thought possible.

THE ALIEN-INVASION
STRATEGY

The next strategy is to look at your idea from an outside point of view. We call this the alien-invasion strategy. When using the alien-invasion strategy, you take the problem statement and imagine solving it the way an alien might. Imagine you are an alien who just arrived on Earth. You have no background of Earth's customs, traditions, or the intricacies of how society works. What solutions could you come up with to solve the problem?

While doing this strategy, take a look at the solutions and evaluate each for stigmas. Can these ideas actually work? Which stigmas need to be held true and which could be erased? After everyone has come up with their ideas, go through the stigmas just as you did with the wild-imagination strategy.

Here's an example in action. Say a problem statement comes up: "Parking in the nearest city is extremely variable." Sometimes it's full when there's an event going on. Other times, 60 percent of spaces are available. An alien may look at this problem and say:

- Why do spaces always have to be parking spaces?
- Maybe we can make gardens that can slide over the parking spaces for people to walk in?
- Maybe we can make a parking area right outside the city and have everyone take public transportation in from the outside of the city?

They may even question why we're using cars in the first place, since it's not the fastest way to get around.

Put the new ideas you create when thinking like an alien on the board. Then list the stigmas and vote on them to identify which are stigmas and which are requirements. So, a stigma might be that a parking spot needs to be a parking spot 100 percent of the time. Well, we found that you could have a garden slide over it or use the space part of the time for something else, so this is a stigma and not a requirement.

EXERCISE 26:

THE ALIEN-INVASION STRATEGY

Instructions: Use the alien-invasion strategy to solve the idea of highways having too much traffic. Make sure you write down the stigmas and requirements along the way.

Outcome: Sometimes, forcing yourself to take a look at something from an outside point of view helps you see problems differently than you normally would. This can help you identify stigmas and solve your problems more effectively!

CHANGE THE ORDER

Another strategy is to change the order of the steps you take in approaching a problem. In the previous strategies, we looked at each stigma one at a time, found it, evaluated it, erased it, or made it a requirement. The other way is to find as many potential stigmas as you can, then evaluate them all, then erase them. For example, instead of finding stigma A and evaluating it, then finding stigma B and evaluating it—you could list 25 stigmas and then evaluate each one by one. Sometimes if you're on a roll, it's easier to just continually develop your stigmas. Talk to your team and see what's easier for them or what's easier for you in your everyday life.

CONCLUSION

These strategies can help you when trying to overcome stigmas and resolve a problem. Writing your stigmas down can be extremely helpful during your problem-solving exercises. Knowing what is truly a requirement and what is just a stigma enables you to explore all of the possibilities before deciding on a solution to a problem.

CHAPTER 11

ERASING LONG-HELD STIGMAS

Sometimes, the stigmas we have are things we've grown up with, things that our whole family or society believes in. For example, that dinner should be the biggest meal of the day, that you should always take your shoes off in someone's home, or that traffic lights are the safest option for an intersection of four streets. Erasing stigmas you've had for a long time, maybe even since childhood, can be challenging. Changing these long-held thoughts or beliefs takes time. You could be erasing years of ingrained beliefs. So how do you go about it? In this chapter, we'll look at how to overcome these stigmas.

HOW TO ERASE A STIGMA

There are four steps to erase a stigma or long-held belief:

1   Noticing the stigma
2   Starting to erase the stigma
3   Staying consistent
4   Noticing when you've finished

STEP 1:
NOTICING THE STIGMA

The obvious first step is noticing your long-held stigmas. These might be hard to spot, because they're things you've believed for a long time, and because your whole family, business, or society might believe them too. The stigma-finding exercises and identifying your habits will help you with this task.

However, don't aim to erase all of your long-held stigmas at once and just expect them to go away quickly. Once you've identified your long-held stigmas, pick a couple and work toward erasing them. Then move on to the others later. Don't give yourself an extremely difficult task all at once. Breaking it down helps you see your progress.

STEP 2:
STARTING TO ERASE THE STIGMA

Once you've picked the long-held stigmas you want to work on, it's important to pick a date to start erasing them. Pick a day you're comfortable with. Maybe you want to give yourself a week or are willing to start erasing them tomorrow. However, don't set the date too far in the future, as you might forget it or simply be putting off starting the task.

When the day comes, then start erasing them. To do this, take your stigmas and apply them to the problems you find daily to test how important they are.

STEP 3:
STAYING CONSISTENT

The next step is to stay consistent with it. Every day, take five minutes to think of five solutions that specifically involve breaking your stigma. Consistency is hard, but working on erasing stigmas a little bit each day will help you fully erase them. Try to practice erasing your stigmas at the same time each day. Continue to do this daily with the stigmas you want to erase, and your mind will eventually adjust.

STEP 4:
NOTICING WHEN YOU'VE FINISHED

The final step is to spot the endpoint. You need to identify when you have successfully erased your stigma. This endpoint should be based on how you feel, not on a specific amount of time that's passed. When you're trying to solve a problem and you don't consider your stigma to be a necessary requirement for a solution, that's when you know you've successfully erased it.

AN EXAMPLE OF
ERASING A STIGMA

Let's look at this practice. Say you've identified a problem: "My job is sapping the life out of me." A long-held stigma that might hold you back from seeing all of the options is: "I must maintain a consistent nine-to-five job to make the money I need and to be successful." This is a stigma you may have developed because your family or society believes it. But it limits you when considering your career options.

In step one, you notice the stigma. This is often the hardest part, because it's something you've believed for a long time and it's been ingrained in your thinking. Since you're unhappy in your current job, you begin to research other jobs and start finding information on people who are making money in unique ways while not sticking to the nine-to-five grind. You realize it's possible to make money and be successful without that grind. Not only that, but you think maybe it will lead to greater happiness. In doing so, you notice your stigma. You realize it's not a requirement that all jobs are a traditional nine-to-five after all. So you decide you want to erase the stigma.

Next, you pick a start date to start erasing it. Breaking a long-held stigma can be difficult, so you do some mental preparation and mark the coming Monday as your start date on your calendar. This gives you a hard deadline that's not too far in the future, but it also gives you some time to prepare for changing this long-held belief.

Monday comes around, and you start erasing the stigma. The first step in erasing the stigma involves research. For example, you might search online to find out about people who have broken the nine-to-five mold. Write down how these people broke the stigma. Maybe you'll find out how travel bloggers make money and escape the nine-to-five grind. Perhaps you'll find out about successful entrepreneurs, chefs, or investors and their unusual lifestyles. The possibilities are endless, but what's important is that you find examples of others who defy the stigma successfully.

The second step is to strategize common ways to erase the stigma. Through research, you've seen the common ways that people break this stigma. Document the strategies they used in your notebook. Next, you need to apply these strategies to yourself. Could you follow one of these strategies to be successful? Could you become a blogger or an entrepreneur? If not, keep researching until you find a method you could follow. You may need to do a little more research. Then start making a plan of action to incorporate the strategy into your life—with small steps every day. Then, get started on actually incorporating your strategy.

You need to stay consistent, so it's a good idea to set an alarm, or maybe do this stigma-erasing work on your daily commute. Choose somewhere you can do it easily without it feeling like too much of a commitment. Keep working on it every day, and your stigma will disappear faster than you might imagine!

LEARN AT YOUR OWN PACE

You might have heard of the 21-day rule. The basic premise is that it takes 21 days to form a habit and 21 days to erase a habit—and as we've seen, our stigmas often lead to habits. However, this is not universally true with every single habit and every single person, so don't give yourself a strict time limit.

Some stigmas are harder to erase than others. Each individual is different, their brains work differently, and it may take them different amounts of time to adjust. Therefore, if you still find yourself participating in the same stigmas after 21 days, that's okay—just continue to work on erasing them. Sometimes it can take months.

CONCLUSION

Long-held stigmas are hard to break because you've believed in them for a long time, and possibly because they've been ingrained in you by your friends, family, or society. However, with a lot of commitment and consistent work in discovering how these stigmas aren't true, you can open your mind to a world of possibilities.

CHAPTER 12

CHALLENGING THE STATUS QUO

So, you've started to erase your everyday stigmas, the ones that affect you specifically when you're problem-solving, and those long-held stigmas. But to really influence and improve the way our everyday world operates, we must challenge the status quo. The status quo means "the way things are done" or "the current state of affairs." In both the wider world and individual societies, there is an underlining status quo. In society, this includes the social structure and the values people hold. In this chapter, we'll look at why we need to break the status quo.

HOW TO SPOT THE STATUS QUO

To challenge the status quo, first you need to identify it. The status quo represents what's normal, common, and expected. Sometimes, these rules can be hard to notice, but a good question to ask is, "What habits do most people share?" or "What do most people consistently do every single day?" Consider both your personal life and business. Another good question is, "What is something that most people believe?" A simple example could be that most people check their email first thing in the morning, or a more serious example could be that a marketing firm has been targeting the same market the same way for over five years. Finding these key inefficiencies caused by the status quo can lead to extreme success.

One of the most common phrases I hear when asking questions related to potential issues within a business is, "We've always done things this way." This is a giant red flag! Anything you do just because *it's always been done that way* is an area begging to be updated. It's another way of saying, "We don't have a good reason why we do it this way—we just usually do it this way, so that's why we do it this way."

Another way to look at the status quo is by asking what rules and guidelines you or others follow to make sure everything runs as normal—either in business or home life. Being able to list these rules will help you identify things that are part of the status quo there.

The key is looking out for rules, guidelines, beliefs, or habits that most people in your business, home life, or society follow. These indicate the status quo. Sometimes, the beliefs or habits you notice are things that only you follow. In these cases, it's not a common status quo you're dealing with, but your own status quo, and you may need to go back to the previous chapters on erasing your personal stigmas (chapters 8 and 11). To challenge the status quo, you're looking for the things most people do or believe.

EXERCISE 27:
IDENTIFYING THE
STATUS QUO

Instructions: Examine your personal or business life, and find examples of the status quo. Then write them down. Think about other people and society, and see whether you can come up with 10 things that people and society do because "Society has always done it this way" or "We have just been doing it this way for a long time."

1

2

3

4

5

6

7

8

9

10

THE STATUS QUO
IN BUSINESS

In the world of business, there's a simple rule you can use to identify the status quo. I call it the "extended traffic light rule." In business, things are bound to change and improve over time. So, if you've been doing something the same way for a long time, there is a high chance that you're falling behind.

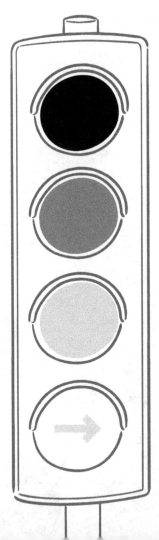

10+ years: This is the red zone. If you haven't made changes in more than 10 years, this area is in extreme danger of becoming obsolete or irrelevant.

5-10 years: You have a yellow light. This is the yield zone. If you haven't changed a process or innovated in 5-10 years, you might not be able to keep up when new products, services, and systems come along.

2.5-5 years: You have the green light for change if you've been doing something the same way for 2.5-5 years. It's the right time to examine the process and innovate.

0-2.5 years: You have a right turn signal. It could be time to change direction if a good idea comes along.

WHY SHOULD YOU CHALLENGE THE STATUS QUO?

Humans are incredibly routine. We are creatures of habit. Although this has its advantages, it often makes innovating hard. Innovating is crucial to the development of our world, so it's important not to be stopped by the status quo. If you can positively break the status quo, this could lead to ground-breaking success.

Challenging the status quo effectively can lead to game-changing ideas. It's important to examine society closely, because we don't change as fast as the human brain can come up with effective ways to change. Challenging the status quo can help you find areas in life where you need to make real progress and create change.

Some people believe you should follow the rules to be successful, but successful people regularly break the rules! They push society to its limits, and they try to do things that people never thought were possible. It's important to try to break these rules in a positive way. When you break the rules and push the limits, it can lead to innovative and creative solutions. If you see rules that don't make sense to you, then challenge them and question them. It's critical that we don't let the status quo hold us back from innovation.

In business, things that have been done the same way for a long time are ripe for change. For example, if a factory hasn't improved its technology for more than 10 years, it's most likely operating at a disadvantage compared to its competitors.

HOW TO CHALLENGE THE STATUS QUO

It's important to examine your life closely in order to challenge the status quo. Three questions and answers you should look for are:

1   Can I change this status quo?
2   If I can change this status quo, guideline, or rule, does it adhere to the moral, ethical, or legal code?
3   If I change this status quo, guideline, or rule, will it lead to an increase in efficiency?

If you can answer "yes" to all three of these questions, then it's time to challenge the status quo.

CONCLUSION

It can be scary to go against the status quo, but challenging the way things are done is an important part of improving society, creating innovation in business, and making your personal life better. Those who are the most effective at positively challenging the status quo are often the most successful.

SECTION 3

//

CREATING
SOLUTIONS

CHAPTER 13

THERE'S NO SUCH THING AS A CRAZY IDEA

There is no such thing as a crazy idea. Yes, it's true. Crazy ideas help you explore all of the possibilities, challenge your stigmas and boundaries, and be more creative. Having crazy ideas is crucial because they help you flesh out what is necessary and possible when your idea is put into action later. Coming up with crazy ideas is important in the idea process. Sometimes, the crazy ideas turn out to be the most feasible, so don't ever rule them out.

Having a crazy idea can also inspire others. People's ideas bounce off each other's. When someone presents a crazy idea, it might inspire a thought that is of extreme value to the brainstorming and solution process. This is why it's important that all ideas are shared, which we'll look at in more depth in section 5. Say we're brainstorming about creating a new type of tea. Someone suggests the idea that the tea bag should explode in the cup to help spread the flavor. This is pretty crazy, as it would probably make the tea spill out of the mug! But someone else is inspired by that idea and suggests we should make the tea fizzy. A lot of people like carbonation, so this idea might just work. Even though the first idea was crazy, it inspired an idea that could be viable.

If you doubt that crazy ideas are worth pursuing, then just take a look at history—many crazy ideas have worked. The Wright Brothers were dubbed as crazy for trying to build an airplane, but they ended up being successful. If not for ideas that were perceived as crazy at the time, we wouldn't have light bulbs, electricity, the internet, or smartphones.

Keeping crazy ideas around helps you avoid eliminating possible solutions too early. Are your crazy ideas going to work every time? No, probably not, but sometimes an idea that seems crazy might be viable when you dig into it.

In fact, many of the world's biggest companies nowadays are built on crazy ideas. 30 years ago, if someone had told you they wanted to create an online marketplace to sell items and help eliminate physical stores, you would have laughed. But that's what Amazon has become. So, get those crazy ideas written down, because you never know when one might make sense or be an excellent pivot toward your success!

EXERCISE 28:
CALL ME CRAZY

Instructions: You're at a meeting with the leaders of your local community. You have to pitch them five ideas crazy enough they might actually work. What are your five ideas?

1

_____

_____

_____

2

_____

_____

_____

3

_____

_____

_____

4

_____

_____

_____

5

_____

_____

_____

Here is a sample idea. It might make more sense to make our main street entirely car-free. This will give our local community members a place to walk, drum up business for the shops on the street, and allow our community to come off as more attractive to visitors.

EXERCISE 29:
WHAT CAN YOU
MAKE OF CIRCLES?

Instructions: This is a creativity exercise created by IDEO, a creative design firm, who used it as a prompt to get the creative juices going. Here, we have a bunch of circles. Give yourself two minutes to draw as many pictures as you can think of using the circles. If you can come up with more than that, then keep drawing more circles and designs!

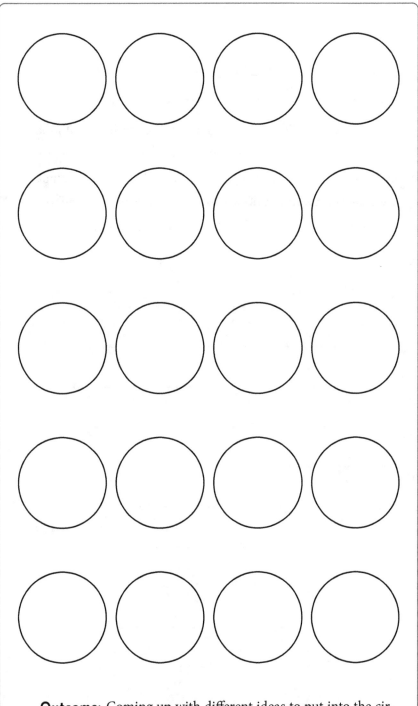

Outcome: Coming up with different ideas to put into the circles will spark the mind and encourage creativity.

EXERCISE 30:
THE WORST COMPANY IDEA

Instructions, Part 1: This game can be fun to do with many people, but it can also be done by yourself. Set a timer for five minutes and write down as many bad business ideas or worst company ideas as you can think of. For example: "smelly, used underwear outlet" or "mattresses made of bee nests." Get creative!

_____

_____

_____

_____

_____

_____

_____

_____

_____

Instructions, Part 2: Now pick one of your favorite ideas. If you're doing this exercise with multiple people, show your partner your favorite worst company. They'll be working with the company you shared, and you'll be working with the company they shared. If you're doing the exercise by yourself, you can work with your own favorite worst company. Now take the idea and pretend you're presenting it to an investor for a new company.

Create a pitch on why this idea will be the next great small business. Get creative in your delivery. During the pitch, discuss what the business is, who would want it, why you would be the best to run it, and anything else you think will help your case. You can do a fake presentation to a friend, group, or someone you know. Feel free to let the audience ask questions when your pitch is done.

_____

_____

_____

_____

_____

_____

_____

Outcome: This drill forces you to present, think on your toes in answering questions, get creative with really bad businesses, and identify what stigmas really exist in an industry. It also forces you to work on your presentation skills and outside-the-box thinking by presenting these bad businesses as potentially profitable ventures.

CONCLUSION

It's not just okay to be crazy out there and creative—it's an important part of reaching for truly innovative ideas. You never know when the next crazy idea might become a reality. Never get discouraged if someone thinks your idea is too crazy!

CHAPTER 14

BRAINSTORMING AND MIND MAPPING

N ow that you know how to identify problems, eliminate your stigmas, and decide which are requirements, it's time to come up with a solution. But how? The starting point in coming up with a solution is a brainstorm or mind map, because these tools enable you to come up with a lot of ideas—and the more ideas, the better! In this chapter, we'll look at brainstorming and some rules for it. We'll also explore mind maps and how they can be customized for your specific purpose.

BRAINSTORMING

We've all heard of brainstorming, but what exactly is it? Brainstorming is the process of coming up with creative ideas and solutions to problems in a rapid free-thinking process. This is why the brainstorming process is extremely important in problem-solving, creativity, ideation, and innovation. Brainstorming can be done alone or in a group. You can brainstorm about almost anything, but to come up with viable and game-changing ideas, you should brainstorm solutions to your specific problems, needs, wants, and questions.

Here are 20 ways to ensure a successful brainstorming session either on your own or in a group:

1   Encourage wild ideas

Welcome all ideas, no matter how crazy. Sometimes, wild ideas can inspire others or you, or they may turn out to be the most logical solutions.

2   Go for quantity

Aim to produce as many ideas as possible. Quantity is the goal. We want to make sure we flesh out every possibility before we move on to the next step, so we need all the ideas we can get.

3   No judgment

It's important not to judge either your own ideas or those of others. Brainstorming is not a time for judgment. Just come up with ideas, and move on to the next ones.

4   Add, don't edit

Don't edit the ideas during brainstorming. If you think something needs to be changed, add a note next to the idea or build another idea. Brainstorming is all about coming up with a lot of ideas, not eliminating ideas.

5 Avoid tangents

Try to stay on task, and don't go too far on tangents. If a tangent comes up, make sure you properly relate it back to the brainstorm—if you relate it, it's not a tangent.

6 Don't worry

Worry often stops people from pursuing ideas. Brainstorming should be worry-free. Be comfortable thinking about or saying your idea no matter who's around or what's going on.

7 No what-ifs or hesitations

Always look forward when coming up with ideas. Don't think, "What if it doesn't work?" If you have a what-if about an idea, don't hesitate—say the idea.

8 Keep energy levels up

Keeping your own and other people's energy levels up can make the brainstorming process more fun or exciting and can encourage ideas.

9 Don't compare ideas

Now is not the time to compare one idea to another. Save that for later.

10 Don't make fun of yourself or others

Don't make fun of another person, idea, or process. Don't make fun of your own ideas or yourself either. All ideas are welcome on the table.

11 One conversation/thought at a time

Try to keep it to one conversation and one thought at a time. You don't want ideas to get lost in a sea of crossed thoughts.

12 Build on other ideas

Build on other ideas that the process creates. Not every idea needs to be completely unique. Sometimes, it makes sense to build on an idea that's already there.

13 You can be visual

You can change it up by drawing ideas or making pictures. If it's easier to be visual, go for it.

14 Treat everyone as equals and have everyone contribute

This is key—no matter what position you're in, everybody needs to be equal. Everyone has ideas, so if people aren't speaking, you're missing out on ideas. Make sure everyone speaks.

15 Keep track of ideas

Don't just talk or think about it—ensure you can go back and reference the ideas later.

16 No negativity

Never, ever be negative in any way. This can drastically hurt the process of brainstorming.

17 No cell phones, computers, or tablets

This is a controversial one, since many people are often on laptops and phones. But try to keep the brainstorming session technology-free to minimize distractions. If something needs to be looked up on the internet, just make a note of it during the meeting.

18 Don't have a rigorous schedule

Putting together a rigorous schedule or agenda hinders people's ability to think creatively. Say you need to brainstorm three topics and you've got one hour. Naturally, you'd think it makes sense to brainstorm each topic for 20 minutes. But to be the most productive, you should brainstorm each topic for however long is comfortable. It may take 35 minutes for the first topic, 15 for the second, and 10 for the third. If you run out of time, you can always schedule another meeting.

19 Don't limit brainstorming to a set time period

Brainstorming should happen around-the-clock naturally. If you come up with another idea when you don't expect it or outside the meeting, that's great! Write it down.

20 Have fun!

Make sure you have fun with it. A fun environment means more ideas.

MIND MAPS

A popular method to document, facilitate, and write down your brainstorming process is called a mind map. A mind map has one idea in the center, with ideas circled in branches off the central topic. These thoughts or ideas have additional thoughts or ideas branching off them. Mind maps can include colors, images, lines, and words. For example, this is a basic mind map about where I should eat dinner:

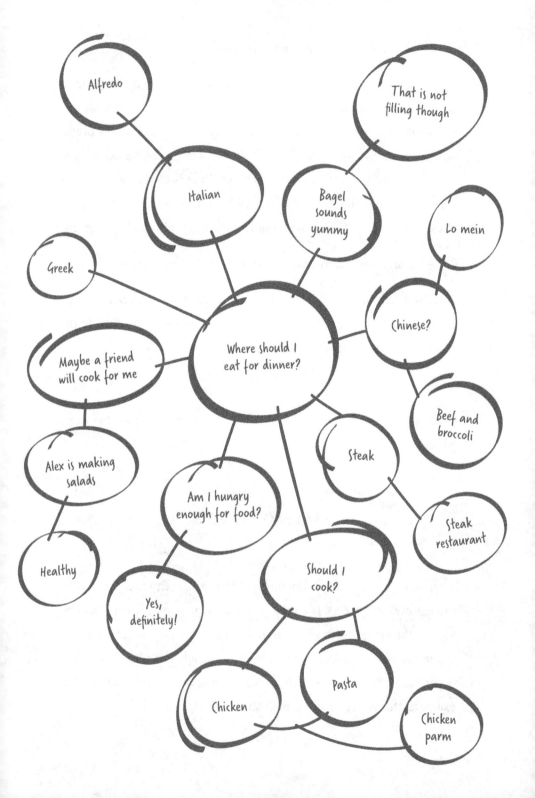

The only rule of mind maps is to have one clear idea to center around. Mind maps are a flexible tool, because you can adjust most aspects, such as size, color, number of lines, number of levels, images, number of words, and structure.

Sometimes, for quick note-taking, it might be easier to do a simple mind map. However, during a brainstorming session, a customized mind map may be more helpful. The more you customize the mind map for your goals, the more helpful it will be. Here is a complex mind map I created:

Mind maps aren't necessary for brainstorming, but they can help to record the information you come up with and encourage creative thinking. Mind mapping can be a useful tool in brainstorming for many reasons, because it:

- Follows the craziness of how humans think. Your mind doesn't think linearly in lists. It thinks of an idea, then it looks to expand on those ideas, and it may jump around to different ideas. A mind map allows you to capture all of that.
- Provides a lot of flexibility, so it's great for a diverse range of problems or ideas.
- Shows the linked relationship between ideas.
- Encourages you to build off other ideas, which is one of the most useful tactics during brainstorming, because adding on to an idea can make it better.
- Is an effective way to get a point across and help people learn, because it's an easy visual tool that enables you to follow ideas across the map.
- Is visual, so it helps with your memory of the exercise.
- Is customized, so it allows you to tailor your thinking, be more efficient in your thinking, and be more effective in understanding your goal.

A BRAINSTORMING TEAM

It's also a good idea to create an effective brainstorming team, or if you're brainstorming alone to find effective people to bounce your ideas off. The key here is building a diverse team of people from varying backgrounds, who bring unique experiences and who think differently. A diverse team of people will use their individual experiences and ideas to solve problems in extraordinary ways that others may not have even heard of.

One of the most controversial guidelines I always suggest is bringing in someone who knows nothing about the topic to help you brainstorm. Someone who doesn't understand or isn't a part of the development process may bring unique ideas to the table. They will also question why you're doing things a certain way. New people tend to examine processes carefully and could raise questions the team hadn't considered. If they ask why you do things a certain way and you don't have a good answer, this may lead to a real conclusion in your brainstorming or solutions. This goes for scientific, business, or life brainstorming situations.

EXERCISE 31:
MIND MAPPING

Instructions: Now you're going to create your own mind map. I've listed three possible topics, so choose one and get creating.

- **Topic 1:** What is a change you can make to forward yourself in your life or career?
- **Topic 2:** If you could create a meal never created before, what would you make?
- **Topic 3:** How can you better keep in touch with your friends and family?

CONCLUSION

From just a simple brainstorming session, you've now come up with multiple ideas to solve your problem—and you probably had fun doing it, right? Practicing mind mapping helps you develop your creative skills and brainstorming documentation skills. The process encourages you to keep pushing yourself to the next level, so keep brainstorming and creating mind maps any time you encounter a problem. By doing this, you'll come up with more ideas that will lead to more creative and innovative solutions than you ever thought possible!

CHAPTER 15

SELECTING
SOLUTIONS

Now that you've come up with many possible ideas to resolve the problem through brainstorming and mind mapping, it's time to look at them as potential *solutions* and not just a lot of random ideas. These ideas will transform into real solutions to your problems, so let's evaluate them and select the best solution for the problem.

Most problems have multiple solutions. This is sometimes hard to grasp. At school or in a job, things often need to be done or answered in one way, but life is much more complicated than that. Often, you can do things multiple ways, and all of these ways can be just as efficient. This means you need to look at your solutions like this too.

Let's take a simple example. Say you identified a problem: "The local road is icy, and I feel it's unsafe to get to where I need to go." You brainstormed and came up with lots of solutions. For example, you could walk, get salt to melt the ice, get snow tires for your car, wait for the weather to clear up, shovel the really icy parts, or not drive at all.

Notice how this one problem has multiple solutions that are all viable? Also, these solutions might even have the same efficiency. For example, it may take you the same amount of time and energy to walk as it would to switch to snow tires and drive. There doesn't have to be one right answer, and it's okay to have multiple solutions.

EXERCISE 32:
MULTIPLE SOLUTIONS

Instructions: Consider the following example. You constantly find yourself barely making your plane when you have business trips. Can you come up with five possible solutions to resolve the problem? You might want to brainstorm or create a mind map to come up with ideas.

1 _____

_____

_____

2 _____

_____

_____

3

_____

_____

_____

_____

4

_____

_____

_____

_____

5

_____

_____

_____

_____

Outcome: Notice there are multiple solutions no matter how difficult or simple the problem is? Don't just stop at the first solution to a problem. If you continue to think and brainstorm, you'll find many more possible options.

CHOOSING THE BEST SOLUTION

So, how do you know which is the best solution? First of all, you should never pick ideas or solutions that you're not passionate about. If you do, you'll run into issues when you have to follow up on your ideas. If you've identified multiple ideas that you feel passionate about or more than one that makes sense, then you need to check whether they're feasible. In other words, you need to pick solutions that you think can actually work. If you're passionate about an idea but you're afraid it might not work, then *don't pick it.* You have to believe in your ideas.

For simple problems, the decision of which solution to pursue might be incredibly quick and easy. In the icy road example, you might feel passionate about walking, because you need to get some exercise. Or you might think putting snow tires on isn't practical because they're underneath a pile of heavy junk in the garage. In these cases, the best solution can be determined by quickly weighing up the options.

However, for complex or dynamic problems, you may need to conduct a more thorough check to see whether each idea is feasible. One way to do this is to break the big problem down into smaller parts until these little problems can be solved with smaller, simpler solutions. You can then combine the solutions together to get one big solution. We'll look at how to combine ideas in the next chapter.

GROUP SETTINGS

What if you're not making the decision between solutions on your own? Or the decision needs to be made in a group? If you're in a group setting, the best suggestion is to hold a vote to decide which solution you move forward with. Not everyone will agree with every idea, but you should try to get two-thirds of the group to agree. If they don't, this is an indication that more discussion is needed.

One way to go about voting is the "Pitch and Post-It" approach. Multiple people will pitch the top ideas in front of everyone else. Everyone has two different colored Post-Its (one color with a value of one and the other color with a value of two). Group members then put the Post-Its on their two favorite ideas, and someone tallies up the totals. If the total for one idea doesn't reach the two-thirds mark, then the group will discuss the solutions in more depth.

At this point, you may choose to conduct a full feasibility check of the ideas—especially if the group feels passionate about multiple ideas. We'll look at feasibility checks for business ideas in section 4.

CONCLUSION

When choosing the best idea or solution, smaller and less complex problems can often be resolved quickly by considering which idea you're most passionate about and which instantly seems the most feasible in the situation. For more complex problems, you can break it down into smaller problems with smaller solutions. If you're in a group setting, you want the majority of people to agree on the idea. If it's close, then you prob-ably need to talk about the ideas in more depth. In the next section, we'll look at how to conduct a full feasibility check for more complex problems.

CHAPTER 16

COMBINING
SOLUTIONS

So, you've got plenty of ideas, but your problem is complex, and no one solution seems to resolve it. One of the best ways to come up with creative ideas for complex problems is by combining possible solutions, that is, taking some of the ideas from your brainstorming exercise and putting them together.

When you're looking at complex problems, it's easier to break them down. Say your problem is: "Our hiring process is too complex." This could be broken down into smaller problems, such as:

1   There are too many stages in the hiring process.
2   The online application system often crashes.
3   The information isn't passed from person to person in the process.

By breaking this large, complex problem down into smaller problems, you could combine the solutions from the smaller problems to solve it.

COMBINING RANDOM ITEMS

Combining random things doesn't always provide viable solutions, but occasionally it leads to a solution, so it's worth a try. It's also an excellent brain warm-up to get ideas flowing and encourage people to be creative. If you're having trouble coming up with creative ideas during the brainstorming exercise, then you can try this out alongside mind mapping or even as an icebreaker before a group brainstorming session.

Say you're a travel company trying to come up with a new business offering. You may want to combine two items to get the ideas flowing, such as an apple and an airplane. There are many random ways you can combine objects to come up with ideas, for example:

- Fresh apples as airline food
- Apple-scented air freshener for airplanes
- Airplanes that give you Apple devices to use for free
- An airline that takes you on a trip to remote apple orchards
- A plane that can transfer plants safely to different locations

Combining two random things or items related to your problem can spark ideas or get the process going. It inspires creativity, because it forces you to think while limiting the field you're thinking about. If you have to just come up with an idea out of nothing, it might seem incredibly difficult because the options are endless, but when you pick two specific items, the range of ideas to choose between is narrower.

Doing this can also help you come up with specific outside-the-box conclusions, because these connections are harder to come up with, especially if the items aren't obviously linked. This process can be done not only with items but also with words, pictures, or anything you can see or think of.

You can apply it to your current problems to get solutions. Most importantly though, combing random solutions helps you practice and train your brain to be innovative. Creatively figuring out ways to combine viable solutions will lead to an even better end solution.

EXERCISE 33:

COMBINING TWO RANDOM ITEMS

Instructions: Now you'll be given some sets of images. For the first two, combine the two pictures to come up with a random idea. The pictures may not be clear or make sense—that's okay. The point of this part is to get your brain operating creatively.

For the second two, combine the pictures to come up with an idea for the industry provided. The goal here is to narrow your mind and get your brain used to coming up with solutions and ideas in a limited area, as this is how real life works.

+ MUSIC INDUSTRY

+ BACKPACK INDUSTRY

Remember, these are just creativity exercises to get the brain going, so they don't have to be perfect!

Outcome: This exercise extends your creativity and stretches your mind by creating connections. This can be helpful in brainstorming and finding solutions. The second exercise forces you to apply these images to industries, enabling you to channel those connections and apply them even more specifically. This random-item combining will prepare your brain to help practice the idea of combining solutions that can work even better together than on their own!

COMBINING YOUR IDEAS

Combining two ideas is a popular and viable way of coming up with solutions. Let's say you have two ideas from your mind map and you're looking to come to one solution. Often, the best answer is to combine them, because this will give you the best of both ideas. When looking to combine two ideas, ask the following questions:

- How can both of these ideas be used in one solution?
- What are the most critical and crucial parts of each idea?
- If the ideas are contradictory, is there a middle ground?

If you're able to combine two good ideas together, this will often lead to one great idea. Let's say you've heard that a storm is coming and you're trying to figure out how to handle a blackout. One idea is to use candles and the other is to use a generator. Combining the solutions means you could use the generator for necessary things like your fridge, so the food doesn't go bad, and for medical devices. Then you can use candles for everything else. This is a viable and efficient solution gained by combining two separate solutions.

This is common practice in the real world. Often, new inventions are created based on an existing solution plus a new solution that the inventor notices. A simple example of this is a suitcase with wheels. While the suitcase has existed for centuries to transport clothes and possessions, in 1970 an inventor named Bernard Sadow was lugging his heavy suitcases through an airport when he noticed somebody easily moving heavy machinery on wheels, and he thought of combining the two. Combining these solutions led to the idea of the wheeled suitcase! (You can read more about his invention in the 2010 *New York Times* article "Reinventing the Suitcase by Adding the Wheel" by Joe Sharkey.)

EXERCISE 34: COMBINING TWO SOLUTIONS

Instructions: Here, you have the problem and two separate solutions. Combine the solutions in the final column to come up with one solution. Some of these will come easily and combine nicely. Others are harder to combine, and you may need to find a middle ground to combine them.

PROBLEM	SOLUTION 1	SOLUTION 2	COMBINED SOLUTION
Running late to work	Buy a faster car	Move closer to work	
Increase sales	Spend more on marketing and promotion	Hire a more skilled marketing team	
Get friends to stop fighting	Have them apologize to each other	Have them stop talking to each other	
Not enough time in the day	Map out and schedule your average day to see whether you can find spare time	Quit your job	
Feeling stressed	Travel somewhere on vacation	Meditate more often	
Want to have more thrills in your life	Make a bucket list	Do something that scares you	
You are doing a poor job of running your team and want the team to perform better	Talk more to your team to find out what is wrong, and practice your leadership skills	Step down as team leader	

Outcome: This exercise shows you that sometimes, combining solutions can be easy, but other times it can be harder. When it's harder, finding a middle ground is important to get a solution. When you are put in tough situations where you have to make difficult decisions, remember that linking solutions or ideas can help you come up with the best options.

CONCLUSION

Combining solutions is one of the most critical parts of idea creation. Often, you can make two really good ideas better by mixing them together. Putting ideas together can enable you to tackle complex problems and bring about more thorough solutions.

FEASIBILITY CHECK

If you've made it this far and you're still struggling to come up with ideas, don't worry. Coming up with ideas and finding solutions takes practice. You just need to continually train your brain to come up with new ideas by following the previous steps. You can pause here if you want and keep working on coming up with ideas, or go to chapter 26 to stimulate the idea-creation process.

CHAPTER 17

THE FEASIBILITY CHECK

L et's say you or your group is passionate about multiple ideas—how do you decide which idea is the best? This is where you need to do a feasibility check. The feasibility check questions for both business and personal ideas are:

- Do you want to pursue it?
- Is there are a market for it?
- Does the market want it now?
- What resources do you have?

First, let's take some ideas you came up with and start evaluating them. List all the ideas, and ask yourself, "Which do I want to pursue most?"

Is there one that seems more exciting to you? If so, mark it. Next, ask yourself, "Which of these ideas do I want to do now?" Are there some ideas you're passionate about but don't want to pursue right now? Understanding this will help you decide which ideas to pursue first. Lastly, ask, "Which ideas can I get the highest-quality resources for in a reasonable time frame?" The idea you want to pursue most right now and can get the highest quality of resources for should be the solution you move forward with.

If you end up with multiple solutions that pass the feasibility test, then you have two options. The first is to rework it and think more deeply about each idea. This might involve researching and finding out more about the ideas. By exploring and researching the ideas, you can add to each idea and understand it better. Then ask the questions again, and one idea should leap to the front. If not, then lean toward the idea that you're most passionate about—because we work the hardest on the things we care most about.

CONCLUSION

Putting ideas through the entire process of the feasibility check is critical. It can save you a lot of time and forces you to think through each of your ideas. You can do a feasibility check for both a personal idea and a business idea. As we move on, we'll do a feasibility check for each type of idea and see how the process is different. We'll also consider what questions are critical and how to go about tackling them to ensure success.

PERSONAL IDEA FEASIBILITY CHECK

CHAPTER 18

DO YOU
WANT TO
PURSUE IT?

Now that you've come up with possible solutions to your problems, how do you decide whether they're good solutions? You do a feasibility check. The first question to ask yourself when doing a feasibility check on a solution for your personal life is, "Do I want to pursue it?" In this chapter, we'll look at this question and how to answer it.

WHY DO WE NEED PERSONAL LIFE SOLUTIONS?

Before we get started, let's look at why it's important to implement personal life solutions in the first place. *Your life is the only thing you can totally control.* Your goal should be to make your life as enjoyable as possible. To do this, it's important to continually evaluate your life and implement changes that can improve it. To improve your personal life, you need to identify problems, wants, and needs, and come up with ideas that will address each to make things better on the whole. This way, you'll make sure you're living your life to the fullest, rather than living one you're unhappy or only reasonably satisfied with.

DO YOU WANT TO PURSUE THE IDEA?

Okay, let's say you've come up with a great idea that could improve your personal life. To feasibility-check the idea, ask yourself, "Do I want to pursue it?" For example, you identified a problem that you're not getting enough done in the day. Your idea is to start getting up an hour earlier to get more done. Do you want to pursue it? Does it make sense to pursue it? Your mind will most likely give you three possible thoughts:

1   Yes, I definitely want to pursue the idea.
2   I'm not sure whether I want to pursue the idea.
3   No, I definitely don't want to pursue the idea.

Thoughts 1 and 3 are easy to identify and work with.

- **Thought 1:** If you're truly passionate about something, you want to do it, and it will make you happy, then you should **do it.**
- **Thought 3:** If you're not passionate about something, and it won't make you happy, then **don't do it.** It's that simple.

But what happens if you're in the middle—if your brain gives you thought 2? In this case, you can follow a three-step process to decide:

1   What do you value?
2   What makes you happy?
3   What are the pros and cons of the idea?

WHAT DO YOU VALUE?

The first step is taking a look at what you value. If you're not sure whether you want to pursue an idea, then you need to consider what is important to you in your life. This comes down to your underlying morals and values, since they influence why you do the things you do.

Have you ever tried to map out your values? Have you ever tried to dig deeper and ask yourself what makes you happy in life? If someone asked you what rules you live your life by, what would you say? If I asked you to sit down and list 25 things that are of high value to you right now, could you do it? Maybe it's your family, your ability to think creatively, your work, or something else? To choose the right solutions for your life, you need to make sure you understand what is of high value to you.

EXERCISE 35:
KNOW WHAT YOU VALUE

Instructions: Write down and rank the 25 things you value most in life.

1 _____

2 _____

3 _____

4 _____

5 _____

6 _____

7 _____

8 _____

9 _____

10 _____

11 _____

12 _____

13 _____

14 _____

15 _____

16 _____

17 _____

18 _____

19 _____

20 _____

21 _____

22 _____

23 _____

24 _____

25 _____

Outcome: It's important to regularly do self-analysis and understand what you value. This list isn't static—it's active. Things will change in your life, and what you value will change over time and at different points in your life. Keeping track of how important things are to you will make you better at making decisions about which ideas and solutions align with your life.

WHAT MAKES YOU HAPPY?

Once you understand what is of high value to you, you need to know what makes you happy. We should all do the things that make us happy in the long run, but to achieve these things, we need to consider our short-term happiness too. Happiness typically comes from following your values, but how this looks in practice depends on whether you're looking at the short term or long term. For this reason, it's important to keep two happiness lists: a daily list and a long-term list.

The daily list enables you to focus on your current life and how you can make yourself happy *every single day,* rather than just aiming for long-term happiness and making yourself miserable in the short term. You can't just shoot for long-term happiness alone. You need to live with happiness every single day. Focus on the little things each day that can make you happy. These small things will improve your happiness overall and allow you to enjoy each day. It's important to focus on each day as if it could make a serious change in your life.

In the morning, think about what five things will make you happy today, then do them throughout the day. The joy will pay off. For example, my five things today are:

1 Read a news article about a topic I am passionate about.
2 Have a coffee while I sit and relax my brain for five minutes.
3 Jump rope and exercise for 45 minutes.
4 Wake up earlier than normal and watch the sun rise through my window.
5 Spend some time talking to my brother to catch up and see how he's doing.

EXERCISE 36:

FIVE HAPPY

THINGS A DAY

Instructions: List five things you can do to make yourself happy today:

1 _____

2 _____

3 _____

4 _____

5 _____

It's important to note, things that could bring short-term happiness are not always the same as things that will make you *fundamentally* happy. What will ultimately make you happy should hold some sway with your day-to-day choices too. Fundamental happiness is typically related to your core values or what is really important to you. It therefore might influence your five daily happiness things. For example, if chocolate makes you happy in the short term, but your core value is being healthy, then chocolate won't make you fundamentally happy. Or you could compromise and switch to a healthier option such as dark chocolate. It's important to understand what makes you happy, because that's what should drive your actions.

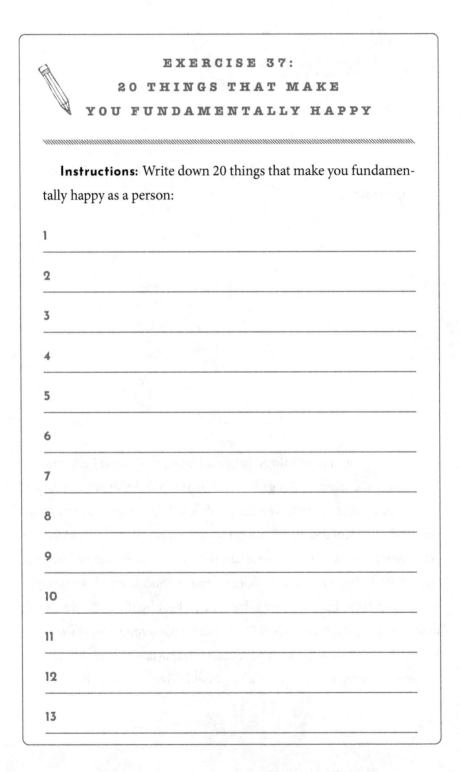

EXERCISE 37:
20 THINGS THAT MAKE
YOU FUNDAMENTALLY HAPPY

Instructions: Write down 20 things that make you fundamentally happy as a person:

1 _____

2 _____

3 _____

4 _____

5 _____

6 _____

7 _____

8 _____

9 _____

10 _____

11 _____

12 _____

13 _____

14 _____

15 _____

16 _____

17 _____

18 _____

19 _____

20 _____

Outcome: Understanding what makes you fundamentally happy will help you lead a happier life, make better daily decisions, and decide whether an idea is worth pursuing or not. It's worth noting that if your values end up changing, then this list can change too, and that's okay.

WHAT ARE THE PROS AND CONS?

After you've decided what makes you happy and what your values are, go back to your idea. If you're still unsure whether you should pursue it or not, make a list or chart of pros and cons. Pros-and-cons charts can be incredibly simple, or they can be colorful and visual. If a pro or con relates to your values, mark it as more important. If it doesn't, mark it as less important. Because you know your values and what makes you happy, writing out the pros and cons will be much easier. One example could be making a rating system for each pro, giving it a score of importance of 1-5, and doing the same for each con. Then add up the total score for each.

If the pros are greater in value than the cons, then go ahead with the solution. If the cons are greater in value than the pros, then don't pursue that solution. Continue to do this, and weigh the pros and cons until there are more of one than the other. If you're not sure about one of the options, then do more research, as that will often lead to more conclusions.

EXERCISE 38:
THE PROS-AND-CONS CHART

Instructions: Think about an idea you currently have that will change your life, but that you're not sure whether to pursue. Create a pros-and-cons chart about the idea. Also feel free to score the pros and cons to better understand how important each pro and con is to you.

CONCLUSION

We should always make decisions to pursue ideas and solutions that will lead us toward long-term happiness. Understanding our values and the things that make us happy will make it easier to know which ideas we should pursue.

CHAPTER 19

WHAT IS STOPPING YOU?

Now that you have an idea you want to pursue, and it's in line with your values, and it will make you happy—can you actually do it, or are there outside forces stopping you? Sometimes, we need resources such as people or things to help us implement the idea. In this chapter, we'll look at the resource aspect of the feasibility check.

There are four questions to ask yourself when making improvements to your life:

1   Can I do this myself?
2   Who do I know who could help me with this?
3   Are there outside entities that can help?
4   What is stopping me from pursuing this idea now?

First, you need to identify whether you can implement this idea in your life by yourself. You have power over your own actions and your life, so you may be able to implement a lot of ideas on your own. Many of the ideas that may improve your life are things you can *just do.* You are the captain of your own ship, so analyze the idea to see whether you can execute it on your own.

The next question is whether you know anyone who can help you get the idea off the ground. Tell a friend or family member your goals and ideas. This will dramatically increase your odds of achieving them. If you can't accomplish your ideas or goals single-handedly, don't be afraid to ask for help. People want to help others they care about. Never be afraid to ask for help, since a little help from others can carry you a long way!

The next question to tackle is whether outside entities can help. If so, identify them. Are they worth paying for? Are their services helpful? Sometimes, outside entities or businesses can help you accomplish your goals. You just need to decide whether that outside help is worth pursuing. Feel free to create a new pros-and-cons chart to help you decide this.

Lastly, one of the most important questions is: "What is stopping me from pursuing this idea now?" This is critical. Often, people's reasons for not going after their goals don't make sense or might not even hold true.

One way to find out whether something nonsensical is stopping you is an exercise called "climb the wall." You take an image of a wall and a rope. You write your challenge on the wall. Above the rope, you write how you would beat that challenge or get over the wall. This method also allows you to track your progress as you overcome your challenges. The following example is about whether or not I can start a business.

EXERCISE 39:

CLIMB THE WALL

Instructions: Create a climb-the-wall exercise for an idea you want to pursue but feel that something is stopping you. This could be a goal where you feel you're holding yourself back.

GOAL: START A BUSINESS

CHALLENGE 4:

I am not a good
enough salesperson.

CHALLENGE 3:

I do not have
enough time.

Take a sales class online/
bring a salesperson onto
my team/set up a business
model so I will not be
personally selling

CHALLENGE 2:

I do not have
enough money.

Switch my job to remote so I can
manage time more efficiently/create a
schedule of goals and time to
organize/outsource some work

CHALLENGE 1:

I do not have
enough experience.

Get a loan/obtain money from
family, friends, or fools/look for a
venture capitalist/find an angel
investor

I got
this!

Bring on a partner/receive further
education/self-teach using online resources

CONCLUSION

Sometimes, when you write down challenges and force yourself to think of a way to overcome them, they don't feel so big after all. Often, you're your own biggest threat. Don't hold yourself back. Use the resources and knowledge you have to propel yourself toward your goals.

BUSINESS IDEA FEASIBILITY CHECK

Now we're going to look at business ideas. The next three chapters consider ideas related to a business or company environment or the creation of a new business or company. We'll go through a business feasibility check to ensure that the idea is valid. Feel free to skip this section if it doesn't currently apply to you.

IS THERE A MARKET FOR THE IDEA?

When feasibility-checking a business idea, we need to ask three questions. The first question is: "Is there a market for the idea?" There's little point in taking forward a business idea if there's no market for it. So in this chapter, we'll look at the potential market for your idea.

What is market research? You might have heard of the term before, and you might have mental images of being asked to fill out a survey or provide some feedback on a product. That's just one type of market research. It actually includes any and all research that looks into your industry, customers, solution, product or service, and the delivery of the product or service.

WHO IS THE MARKET?

To understand who your market is, you need to ask two questions:

- Who would want the idea or solution to the problem?
- Who is facing the problem that your idea solves?

A market is a specific and defined group of people. It's important to be able to effectively find people who would want your idea. A market isn't necessarily outside the business either. If it's an internal business problem you're solving, then the market may be your employees or the accounting department.

There may be multiple people who could use that idea, but there should always be a leading market. When searching for your market, you need to check who is facing the problem that your idea best solves and who is most affected by the problem you're solving. If a specific and defined group faces an issue you're planning to solve, then you're on track.

TALK TO YOUR MARKET

Once you identify your market, talk to people in it. See whether this solution is something they would *actually want*. There are many ways to do this. Physically go out and talk to people, send out online or paper surveys, and call people. This can be as large-scale or small-scale as your business allows, but the goal is to get as much feedback as possible on the idea from the people who would use it—your potential customers.

You can also ask members of the market about feedback you've received from other people. Doing so can help you decide whether the feedback applies across the board, or whether it's only relevant to a few customers. For example, say you run a jump rope company. One customer gives you a suggestion on changing your grip to a different material. Rather than immediately changing it, you should go to other customers to see whether they like the material, so you can get statistically significant feedback.

TALK TO PEOPLE IN YOUR INDUSTRY

While it's most important to talk to your actual market and your potential customers, the second most important group you need to speak to is those in your industry. You need to understand the industry you're in (or entering), and to do this you need to talk to people who work in your industry. To get the best information, ask people in your industry, but don't ask your direct competitors. The ideal is people who worked in the industry but are now retired, particularly people who are interested in mentoring you. These people will be knowledgeable in the area but not involved anymore, so they're not a potential competitor. Getting feedback from people who are familiar with your area will help you refine your idea.

TALK TO PEOPLE OUTSIDE YOUR MARKET

Finally, you should talk to people outside your market or industry—to get a "breath of fresh air" opinion. This is the third most important group, so try speaking to people from this group every once in a while to get a different opinion. People who don't know the industry from the inside may have a unique view, so they'll be able to provide feedback or ideas you may not have thought of. You never know where the best advice may come from. Identify someone whose thought process you like, then reach out to them to connect and explain the problem or solution.

If your market doesn't want your idea, then you should go back to the drawing board. People are the key to your success, and if your market doesn't want it, then the idea will most likely fail. If this happens, you can do one of two things: you can change the idea or change the market. If a market doesn't want your idea, go back to the brainstorming phase. Also see whether your idea is too complex. We can often simplify the idea to the minimum viable idea and still have success.

WHAT MARKET RESEARCH TELLS YOU

As mentioned earlier, market research includes any and all research related to the delivery of your solution, and this includes the industry, the customers, and the solution itself.

You can gain two possible insights from market research. Either your potential customers like your idea and want your solution to their problems, or they don't. If they do, ask them for feedback to see how you can improve the idea. If you get repeated feedback that changes are required in one particular area, make sure you edit your idea or solution.

If they don't like the idea, there are two possible reasons. First, you may be talking to the wrong market. In that case, re-evaluate the solution or idea and see whether a different group of people would want this product or service. This re-evaluation can lead to a different market. The second reason is that the idea or solution itself doesn't add value, meaning you may need to re-evaluate the idea, combine it with another solution, or go back to the idea-creation stage. In order to pass this stage of the feasibility check, you need to find a clear market segment that indicates they like the idea and would buy it.

Your goal from the feedback is to find out whether you have everything necessary to make the idea work or whether you do need to do more work on the idea. You want to know the minimum viable idea you could launch that will be successful.

MINIMUM VIABLE IDEA

So, what is a minimum viable idea? A minimum viable idea means the minimum scope you can launch that will solve the problem. The minimum viable idea will require the least amount of resources to solve the problem. You can then build from there. But why look for minimum viable ideas? Why not take a new idea to the max? The reason is for efficiency. Often, we naturally add things to our idea that aren't necessary. This can be time consuming and expensive to carry out.

We need to find out the minimum necessary to launch the idea, as this enables us to move forward with the solution in the fastest and most efficient way. Once you find out from your market what is absolutely necessary for them, then you have the minimum viable idea you can move forward with.

You need to identify two factors when creating a minimum viable idea.

1   What is my differentiator—what makes my idea special?
2   What is necessary to the idea for it to work?

When looking at your differentiator, you need to identify what makes your idea different from all other ideas. Say you have a problem: "My feet are always cold in my entryway to my home." Therefore, you have a new idea for a rug. You want it to have a warmer to keep your feet warm when you're walking on it, and you want it to have tassels and be multicolored. Additionally, you want a checkered design, and you want to ensure it's one of the softest rugs possible.

So, what is your differentiator here? Let's go back to the root of the problem—your feet are cold. Therefore, your differentiator is what problem this solves, as it makes your product different from other rugs. The minimal viable idea here is that the rug needs to have a warmer.

Now let's take a look at the second question. What is necessary for the idea to work? Does it need to have a checkered design? Does it have to be softer than all other rugs? Does it require multiple colors and tassels? All of these things are auxiliary add-ons to the idea. Therefore, they're not necessary for the idea to work.

There is no one minimum viable idea for any solution. There are tons of possible ideas. The important point is that if you're going to move forward with an idea, make sure it's viable and requires the minimum amount of work, because this will lead to lower costs, shorter lead times, and the lowest risk.

EXERCISE 40:

TALK TO PEOPLE

Instructions: Talk to three people around you about a business idea you have. Discuss it with them, get their feedback, and see whether you need to re-evaluate or edit the idea. Aim for at least three customers: two people in the industry and one outsider. See whether your idea will develop or change, and create a minimum viable idea (more on that later).

CONCLUSION

You won't be able to move forward with an idea without a clear market. So, you need to do market research, but remember that this is more than just talking about the idea with your customers. It's also important to talk about the idea with those in the industry and even outsiders to make sure you get plenty of feedback on the idea and have truly looked at it from all sides.

CHAPTER 21

DOES THE MARKET WANT IT NOW?

Time is the one thing outside of everyone's control. Timing is tricky—especially in business. You may have the best idea in the world, but if people aren't ready for it, then the idea will fail. You know there's a market for your solution and that they want it, but do they want it now? In this chapter, we'll look at the part of market research that shows you whether your market wants the idea *now*.

HOW PEOPLE ADOPT AN IDEA

Bill Gross, the founder of the Idealab incubator, gave a TED Talk called "The Single Biggest Reason Why Startups Succeed" (2015) where he talked about an experiment he performed. While working at Idealab, he conducted a survey of 200 companies to examine five factors involved in the success of startups. These were: funding, the idea, the team, the business model, and timing. The results showed that timing accounted for 42 percent of a company's success, which was more than any other factor. Of course, it's important to have all five in place, but if you make sure your market wants it now, that will seriously increase your chance of success. So, how do you know when the timing is right?

In 1962, Everett Rogers published his first book, *Diffusion of Innovations*, named after his theory. In this book, he shows the rate at which people will adopt a new idea. The darker line is the rate of market share percentage over time. Market share is the percentage of customers in your market who have bought your product or service or a competitor's product or service. The lighter line is the number of people who adopt the idea over time.

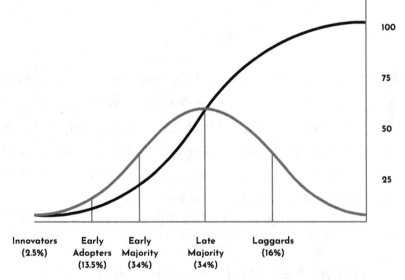

(In *Diffusion of Innovations*. By Everett M. Rogers. Free Press, 2003, 281.)

As you can see, the line is curved. This means that more and more people will adopt the idea over time. It doesn't happen all at once. In any industry, when you launch an idea, there will be innovators who want to try it as soon as possible. Next are the early adopters—people who aren't on the cutting edge of the industry but understand the idea and are willing to adopt it earlier than most. Then there's the early majority section, who will purchase the product or service once the idea is tested and understood. The late majority are people who will buy the product or service after about half of the people around them have purchased it. Finally, the laggards are the last people who pick up on the product or service.

THE TIMING FACTOR

Understanding the timing factor is important, because it can help you discover where your potential customers are on this scale and whether they want this product or service right now. Let's say your idea is a machine that can modify people's genes. It's a great idea and may have a positive impact on the world. However, it wouldn't have much success in a large-scale market, because at this time very few people would be ready to adopt such technology. The innovators section only makes up 2.5 percent, meaning you wouldn't have a big market for your idea. This works the same way in reverse. If a new typewriter were invented, very few people would adopt it, since hardly anyone uses typewriters anymore.

The speed at which an idea and a company moves through the line is based on outside factors. In some industries, things are adopted quickly, while for others, it takes much longer to move from stage to stage. For example, fads and some fashions move quickly through the innovation curve, while very complex systems or products could take much longer, such as a medicine using a new chemical compound.

It's important to find out how quickly your idea would potentially move down this line to determine whether your idea is valuable. This is also part of your market research stage. While you're researching your industry, you should check how mature it is. The older and more mature your industry, then typically, the further along it will be on the innovation curve.

WHAT STAGE IS YOUR INDUSTRY IN?

So, the first step is taking a holistic look at the industry you're in or entering to determine where it falls on the industry lifecycle scale. The following graph shows the stages of the industry lifecycle and how these stages are reflected in sales. In the introduction phase of the scale, people are just starting to understand the industry. In the growth phase, the industry is proven and experiencing massive growth. In the maturity phase, the industry is peaking. In the decline phase, the industry is dwindling away.

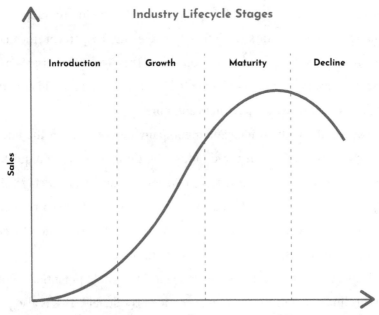

Industry Lifecycle Stages

It's important to understand where your industry lies on this scale, as this affects how well your idea will be adopted. If your industry is in the decline stage, you will get fewer customers over time. If your industry is in the growth stage, then you're likely to get more customers over time. If your industry is in the decline phase, this doesn't necessarily mean you shouldn't enter it. If you can innovate in a declining industry, you may still achieve success.

You can find out which stage your industry is in from most market research reports online. Accessing these reports can be expensive though, so you can estimate approximately where your idea falls by asking these questions:

- Is this brand new to the market with not many competitors and not many customers yet?
  If yes: introduction
- Are more and more people rapidly getting involved as customers or companies in the industry?
  If yes: growth
- Is this something that is consistent and that most people in the market just buy generally?
  If yes: maturity
- Is this something that fewer and fewer people in the market are buying?
  If yes: decline

HOW TO GO ABOUT RESEARCH

So, you know which stage your industry is in, and you're happy that there's a good chance of success because the industry is in the introduction or growth phrase—or you have an innovative idea for an industry in the maturity or decline phase. Now you need to understand the timing of your specific product or service in the market. To understand the timing of your product, you need to answer two big questions:

1   Is there any information related to the timing of my industry or competitors that could affect my solution?
2   Are the customers and market ready for my solution?

For the first question, you need to research your competitors online, see what they're doing, and talk to your competitors' customers. You can also look at overall industry news and research for your specific area.

To answer the second question, you need to talk to your potential customers. Surveys are generally the best way to get information on the timing of your product or service and the readiness of your potential market. You can also research online to find out about other similar solutions, when they launched, and how they did.

IF THE MARKET DOESN'T WANT IT NOW

If your market doesn't want your idea now, what should you do? You could keep the idea and wait until the market wants it. Or develop the idea in full, but wait to launch it. You could re-evaluate your idea and change it so the market will want it now. Or you could re-evaluate your market. Maybe a different market would adopt your idea faster if you adjusted the idea?

You can also do other, more drastic things. You can attempt to educate your market to speed up the adoption process. This is hard and can be expensive, but it is an option. You could use a mass marketing campaign to teach people about your solution, such as a viral video or a large advertising campaign. For example, when Boston Children's Hospital first brought out their Bridge-Enhanced ACL repair surgery, they launched a successful video campaign where people going through torn ACL treatment and recovery could learn about the new procedure. This video has produced many articles and additional information so people can become educated on this new potential procedure. If the more drastic options don't work, then you should go back and rework the idea completely.

CONCLUSION

Timing is critical to success in business, so it's important to identify whether your market is ready for your idea. Some of the best ideas fail because they're too early or too late to the game. Understanding timing takes time and research. But when you understand your market and industry, this will lead you toward success.

CHAPTER 22

RESOURCES

The last question to ask when feasibility-checking your business idea is: "Do I have the resources to make my idea happen?" If people want the idea now and you can provide it to them, then you should be successful. But how do you know whether you have the resources to pull off the idea? In this chapter, we'll examine the resource factor.

WHAT ARE RESOURCES?

When it comes to business ideas, what we mean by resources falls under a broad definition. Resources can be people, funding, the physical product itself, or anything else you need to make the idea happen. Evaluating resources for a business idea is not always straightforward, because different types of resources can yield the same result. Take, for example, building an app. You could pay a company to build it, hire someone to build it, or learn how to build it yourself. You don't need all three types of resources to make the app happen, but you'll need to decide whether you have the resources to pay someone or the time to learn.

EVALUATING RESOURCES

When you evaluate the resources you have or will need, you should always ask yourself four questions, as they will help you come up with options for your resources:

1   Can I make it happen on my own?
2   Can I get the resources I need to make it happen in-house?
3   Can I get the resources to make it happen from an external source?
4   Can I find someone who will work with me to make it happen?

The first question means considering questions like: What skills and resources do I personally have? How quickly can I learn the skills? How hard are the skills to learn? How time consuming will it be to learn them? When looking to bring your idea to action, it often makes sense to complete a lot of the resource requirements yourself if you can.

The second question requires you to assess anyone you already have working for your business unless it's a brand-new business idea and you're working on your own. This might be within your team or the wider business. Check out what skills people have—they might have skills you didn't know about.

The third question means considering whether you'll purchase or receive resources from external sources, such as consultants or companies. This can often be used for requirements you plan to outsource in the long term, for example, things you can't afford now or don't need yet, such as accounting. Alternatively, it can be helpful for specific short-term or one-off projects that require specific skills, such as logo design. If you need a resource, can't do it yourself, and don't have the expertise in-house, outsourcing often makes great sense.

Lastly, ask, "Can I find someone who will work with me to make it happen?" A team can be critical in bringing an idea to reality. It may make the most sense to bring someone onto your team to help you build your idea. This might mean finding a business partner if you're working on your own or hiring someone onto your existing team.

MAKING A RESOURCE CHART

To understand the options better, you can create a resource chart for an idea. For example, this is a resource chart for building an app:

IDEA	OPTION 1	OPTION 2	OPTION 3
Build an app	Pay for an external company to build it	Hire someone to build it	Learn how to code and build it myself
Market to customers for low budget	Hire a part-time employee specifically to do marketing	Use cheap social media marketing	Learn do social media marketing myself
Manage finances	Hire an external accountant to manage the finances	Bring a finance person onto the team	Learn how to make financial statements myself
Receive funding to help support the company	Go to a venture capital firm to get investment	Crowdfund to get more money from potential customers	Self-fund and get money from the three Fs (friends, family, and fools)

Using a resource chart allows you to relay all the possible options and the resources you need for each option. You can extend the chart vertically or horizontally. Get creative with your options. Don't forget to use the brainstorming, stigma-erasing, and solution-picking skills from earlier in the book. When you're done laying out all of your options, you can highlight which options make the most sense for you.

EXERCISE 41:

CREATE A RESOURCE CHART

Instructions: Pick an idea you have, or come up with a simple business idea now. Then identify the options and resources you would need to launch the idea.

RESOURCE	OPTION 1	OPTION 2	OPTION 3	OPTION 4

Outcome: Making resource charts can help you better understand your own and your team's capabilities. It will help you understand exactly what resources are necessary to make an idea a reality. It can also help you plan how to launch an idea and come up with the costs.

CAN YOU GET THE RESOURCES?

There are many resources you could use to bring your solution to reality, and creating a resource chart can help you identify the possible options. However, you need to make sure you can actually get hold of these resources for your idea to pass the feasibility check.

If you don't have the resources to pull off an idea, you should ask yourself, "Why is that?"

- Do you not have the right network?
  If that's the case, you could consider networking and keep moving forward.
- Do you not have enough money?
  You could try to find funding and move forward.
- Is the technology not there yet?
  You could wait for the technology, as long as it doesn't affect the timing of the market.

However, there's no easy way to find out how long the technology will take to come out. It involves research and making an educated guess based on your solution, other solutions in your area, and new inventions in general. This research would include finding out how long the technology will take to develop, when your market will be ready to purchase, and where you could get the product or service quickest.

If you can't find the appropriate resources to pursue an idea, it doesn't make sense to move forward with it. In this case, it may be time to go back to the drawing board and rework the idea. See whether you can change it or combine it with another solution that resolves the resource issue. At all stages of the idea process, it's possible that you may need to move back a few or many steps, and that's okay. Be creative in finding resources—don't just go for the obvious ones.

EVALUATE YOUR STIGMAS

When you're doing the feasibility check, it's important to continually evaluate your stigmas and erase them. For example, you might think you don't have access to the resources because a stigma is holding you back, or you might miss a resource option because of a stigma you still have. In this case, you may need an expert in a highly specific field. Since the field is so unique, you may assume this person doesn't exist without even looking! Stigmas can hold you back during the feasibility check, so you may need to re-evaluate them while you're doing your check. A well-thought-out feasibility check can make or break your understanding of the viability of the idea, so make sure it's stigma-free.

CONCLUSION

If you have the resources available either personally or in-house—or you can hire someone externally or bring someone onto the team—then the idea has passed the final test of the feasibility check and you can move forward. Congratulations!

SHARE,
SHARE,
SHARE

thinks differently. You may think this is a bad thing, but it makes humanity a powerful tool. Every single person will view your idea differently, which is a good thing because each person can provide different feedback and give you unique insights from their personal experiences. They can point out issues, benefits, glaring errors, or possible improvements. This allows you to look at your idea from all angles, not just your own or those closest to you.

Don't be shy to ask someone who doesn't seem in a rush to sit down and talk to you about your idea. The hardest thing about having a new conversation is starting a new conversation—once you start the conversation, everything else will go more smoothly.

BUILDING ON IDEAS

Another benefit of sharing ideas is that it gives you the ability to build on them. When you share ideas, people want to give their opinions. As they highlight inefficiencies or aspects that could be improved, you'll be encouraged to expand your thinking about your original idea. Building on ideas can advance your work and take it to the next level.

Consider asking someone you're speaking to questions like "How would you improve this idea?" or "Is there something you think the idea is missing?" to encourage them to build on your idea.

FORMING A PARTNERSHIP

Sharing can also help you form partnerships. When you share an idea with someone, you may inspire them, and they may ask you to form a partnership

CHAPTER 23

THE BENEFITS OF SHARING

W e're often told that sharing is a good thing in life. But why would you want to share with other people? There are plenty of direct benefits to be gained when you share your ideas. It's important to communicate with other people to get feedback on your idea. In this chapter, we'll look at the reasons why.

A UNIQUE VIEW

Sharing ideas is important because no two people are the same. We all come from different backgrounds, are born in different places to different families, and are raised differently. This means that every single person together. They may have unique skills or be a good fit to work with you. They might become a business partner in the future. It's important to put yourself out there because you never know where you might find the right match to help you bring your ideas to fruition.

CONNECTIONS AND RESOURCES

When you're part of the entrepreneurial or "new ideas" community, it's important to help everyone else out. In these communities, typically everyone is cheering for everybody else. If you're starting a new business, you'll find others who are starting new businesses, and you can share your worries and successes.

However, this also goes for your personal community too, as the people who care about you are cheering you on to help you improve your life. When it comes to new ideas, people are typically excited to help.

Often, people you share ideas with can offer both connections and resources that could be helpful to you. They may hear your idea and be able to connect you with someone who could help. Or they could give you access to resources or information that could help you take your idea forward.

Often, the best way to find a supportive community is by going to events targeted at people coming up with or developing ideas. Whether they're personal ideas or business ideas, there are tons of events on the development of ideas, and the people who show up there are typically looking to give and get help.

HOW TO START
SHARING YOUR IDEA

Before you share an idea, it's helpful to prepare. Do your homework so you have a full understanding of how best to explain your idea, and go in knowing a thing or two about the person you're meeting. Reflect on what they do and how they could possibly help, so you ask the right questions. If you don't already know, do some research to find out. Create a list of questions to keep the conversation going and make sure you touch base on the entire idea.

When you first meet the person, before you dive into what you're working on, try to make a personal connection. Often, this can make a conversation less awkward and more honest, especially if you're meeting someone for the first time. You want the best, most candid feedback you can possibly get, so ensure you make the person feel comfortable in sharing what they actually think. If you're sharing with a friend or someone you know well, you can probably skip this step.

If you don't know where to start, share your trains of thought. More specifically, don't just share an idea you have, but start from the beginning. Explain the problem, how you discovered the problem, what stigmas you erased, and how you got to your idea and solution. This will help explain the problem you're seeking to solve and how you got to your solution. This enables a greater understanding between you and the other person and often leads to more efficiency.

EXERCISE 42:
SHARING

Instructions: You need two people to complete this exercise. Decide who will be person one and person two. For this exercise, you will need 10 coins (or any other circular object). Set them up like this:

Person one starts by reading the instructions for person one. When they're done, they hand the instructions for person two to person two. When person two has finished, they start the timer to begin the exercise.

Person One Instructions:

Person two was given a challenge. You cannot talk to person two unless they ask you to speak. If they ask you to do something, comply. Keep track of the number of times you become frustrated with the process of solving this problem.

Person Two Instructions:

Set a timer for five minutes starting now, then try to solve this riddle:

"Ten coins form a triangle pointing up. Can you move three coins to make the triangle point down?"

You can't touch the coins yourself. If you want to move the coins, you need to get person one to move them for you, and you cannot ask person one to do anything until two of the five minutes have passed. When three minutes remain, feel free to communicate with your partner to solve the puzzle. Make sure person one can see the timer.

Outcome: Most people fail this task, not because they didn't solve it, but because they couldn't cooperate effectively. Why is that? No one likes being told what to do without purpose or meaning. If they understood the "why," they might be able to understand. They can't talk, so they can't communicate or express their feelings, and this is how some people feel in real life too.

The best strategy, which everyone is missing, is simple. Person two shares the entire problem as soon as they can. They ask person one to communicate with them and help them solve it together. This is the best strategy because:

- You will have double the minds working.
- You will be communicating and working together.
- People understand what the problem is instead of being fed a solution.
- They understand your constraints (in this case, time and rules).
- They understand the reason why you're doing it.

This kind of strategy is key because you're giving people the full scope of the situation: the problem, the solution, the strategy, and the constraints. It's important when you share to give the full information, because that will lead to far more useful feedback and discussions.

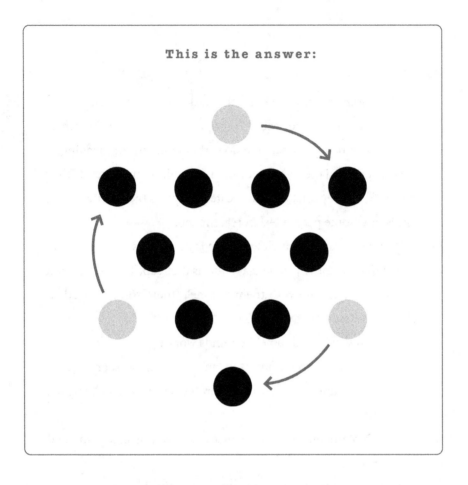

This is the answer:

CONCLUSION

It's important to share your ideas because everyone comes from a different background, so everyone can offer a different view on your idea. It's valuable to understand their opinions and views, as they could point out things you hadn't realized or help you look at your idea from an alternative angle. They may highlight potential problems or benefits you didn't see previously. This can help you build upon and move forward with your idea.

CHAPTER 24

IT'S OKAY TO
SHARE

When you have a great idea, you may want to shout about it from the rooftops immediately! Or you might want to keep it to yourself for a while. When it comes to ideas, there is no bad time to start talking about or sharing them. In fact, you can share and get feedback throughout the entire process. A common time to share the idea is after it has passed the feasibility check, before you move into development.

However, some people are scared or worried about sharing their idea with others. People have two major fears about sharing ideas. One, people are intimidating and could have a negative reaction to the idea. Two, people might steal the idea. These fears are often based on stigmas we have. In this chapter, we'll tackle both of these fears.

NEGATIVE REACTIONS

Let's look at the fear of people having negative reactions, being intimidating, or even being mean when you share your idea and ask for feedback on it. Take a second and imagine being nice to someone. How does it make you feel? Good, right? Would you feel connected to them? For the average person, being nice to someone feels good. Therefore, it's in people's best interests to be nice to other people, because it creates feelings of happiness and a connection. It also makes people feel like they have value.

So in most cases, people will be nice when you share an idea or ask for feedback. If someone shared an idea with you or asked for feedback, you'd be nice, wouldn't you? You'd tell them what works in the idea and maybe give them some pointers on how to improve it. So, why wouldn't people do the same for you?

You also need to show your appreciation and gratitude for the person listening or giving feedback on your idea. Let them know how much you appreciate their expertise and opinions. People like to feel valuable, so treat everyone around you like an expert or potential resource when you share an idea. When I started my first business, I discussed it with elementary school kids—and one of the best suggestions I got was from a fifth grader! You never know where your next idea may come from, so it's important to treat each person like they could be the missing piece of your puzzle. Again, erase your stigmas about who you should share ideas with and who won't be useful to you.

It's also true that people are often nicer if you do something for them. People are more likely to give if they have been given to first. When you're asking for feedback, you can offer something in return. This might be helping them with a problem they're facing or connecting them to someone who can help. Any nice gesture could be helpful. For example, some companies offer entry into a prize draw if customers take part in a survey.

Perhaps you have preconceptions about sharing ideas because your friends or family have ridiculed them in the past. In this case, it's often better to seek out a stranger, especially when it comes to personal ideas. Although this might be uncomfortable at first, a stranger may be more willing to help, and neither of you will have any preconceptions about each other, which can lead to an objective discussion. A great place to do this is a coffee shop, where you can ask whether someone has a minute to review an idea you have. Feel free to strike up a conversation first, maybe about the book they're reading or what they're working on. If they seem up for chatting, you might be surprised to see what a fresh perspective can do for your idea!

In those few cases where you do get negative feedback, don't take it personally, and don't be afraid of it. Negative feedback is just an opportunity to improve, so it's important that you see it that way. When you receive negative feedback, evaluate the root cause of why it's negative, then adjust the solution to make it even better!

IDEA THIEVES

Another common worry, especially in business, is, "What if someone steals my idea?" This concern is less common with personal ideas because if two people choose to live their lives in similar ways, it doesn't cause a problem or competition like it might do in business. However, just because competition is a possibility, this doesn't mean you should avoid sharing your ideas.

You can see that this worry isn't really necessary by looking at some statistics. According to the 2017 Kauffman Index Startup Activity National

Trends, in the United States, 310 people started a business for every 100,000 people in 2017. So, the chance that someone has the same interests as you, relates to and likes your idea, has the skillset to work with your idea, and wants to move it forward is *extremely low.*

What's most important about your idea is **you.** An idea is worth very little on its own, but your personal experience, background, skills, and the way you tackle the problem are all unique to you. So even in the unlikely case that someone wants to steal your idea—chances are they won't be as successful as you. Getting feedback on your idea from others is critical, so it's important to take this small calculated risk and share your ideas!

EXERCISE 43:
SHARE THREE IDEAS

Instructions: Take three ideas you've been thinking about but haven't shared yet. Share and discuss one idea with a friend, one with a family member, and one with a stranger.

Idea:

_____

Who am I sharing it with?

_____

Notes on response:

_____

_____

_____

_____

Idea:
_____

Who am I sharing it with?
_____

Notes on response:
_____

_____

_____

_____

_____

Idea:
_____

Who am I sharing it with?
_____

Notes on response:
_____

_____

_____

_____

_____

_____

CONTROVERSIAL CONVERSATIONS

Talking to other people also means having controversial conversations. This can be tricky because it will make you feel uncomfortable, but it's also necessary. A controversial conversation is a dialogue about a topic that both people are passionate about but disagree on. As humans, we don't like to have these types of conversations, because we build relationships based on our similarities. Actively disagreeing makes most of us feel uncomfortable.

To clarify, a controversial conversation isn't an argument or screaming match—it's a relaxed conversation. In this type of conversation, you dig into *why* people might have a different viewpoint than you. What experiences led them to this view? Understanding the root cause of why they think what they do can be critical to these conversations. This will help you see other people's views in a different light and can inspire curiosity or other new ideas.

EXERCISE 44:
HAVE A CONTROVERSIAL
CONVERSATION

Instructions: Have a controversial conversation with someone you know. Remember to stay calm and make it a discussion, not an argument. Try to understand their reasoning for believing what they do. Don't try to win them over. Write down the insights you gain.

Outcome: Not only will having these conversations be helpful in your idea-gathering phase, but it will help you develop your social skills and give you a better understanding of the world around you.

CONCLUSION

In a nutshell, people are crucial to your success. Other people can help you think differently about problems you're facing, inspire you to come up with new ideas, and encourage you to be curious and ask more questions. The more you talk to people who are different from you, the more you can potentially spot problems or come up with new ideas, because their different viewpoints can shed light on things you hadn't noticed before. If you're scared to share, the only way to overcome these fears is to start sharing!

SO, WHAT NOW?

CHAPTER 25

PLANNING THE SOLUTION

Once you've evaluated your idea fully and it has passed the feasibility check, then it's time to make a plan so you can bring the solution to life. Planning is an important part of turning your ideas into reality, rather than just leaving them as ideas in your head. After all, there's little point in coming up with great ideas but never making them happen!

WHAT TO INCLUDE IN THE PLAN

When you're creating a plan, you need to break the big idea or solution down into specific goals that will enable you to achieve it. When you break your big goals down to a granular level and ensure you know exactly what you need to do to accomplish those goals, then you'll be able to implement your idea. Implementing is a process that takes time. It's a day-by-day set of smaller actions that you continually accomplish to slowly bring larger goals to life.

Establish individual achievements and set yourself a realistic day and time you'll have them completed by. Planning and tracking your goals is important. If you don't give yourself deadlines, you might push off progress again and again. You need to have the self-discipline to accomplish your goals. A goal sheet or map will help with this. In either case, you need to break the big idea down into the following:

1   **Large goals:** Place these on the top.
2   **Medium-term goals:** Add these below.
3   **Short-term goals:** These help you move toward the larger goals.
4   **Daily goals:** These are at the bottom.

In these goal sheets, it's important that all of the goals are **linked**. This means you can see the logical steps you need to take to move closer and closer to your goals. You can also ask people for feedback on your goals, to see whether they make sense. Talking about your goals with others can be extremely helpful.

For example, maybe you have a new idea for a bicycle pedal, and you want to start a business. After looking closely at creating a new pedal design, you decide the medium-term goals. You then split the medium-term goals into smaller goals, for example, "Look closer at doing the design on your computer." The last step is asking, "What specific actions do I need to take today to accomplish my daily goals?"

A goal sheet may look like this:

Goal Sheet

Large goal:

Open an online shop with a newly designed pedal

Date to complete by: 1 year

- **Medium goal 1:** Create a new pedal design
  Date to complete by: 3 months
- **Medium goal 2:** Create social media pages for marketing
  Date to complete by: 1 month

- Small goal 1.1: Find material for the prototype
  Date to complete by: 3 weeks
- Small goal 1.2: Choose a shape for the prototype
  Date to complete by: 2 weeks
- Small goal 2.1: Make a design description
  Date to complete by: 1 week
- Small goal 2.2: Create a design on the computer
  Date to complete by: 3 weeks
- Small goal 2.3: Learn about social media
  Date to complete by: 1 week

Today's goals:

- Find a quiet place to work
- Wake up 30 minutes earlier to work on the designs
- Go to the store and look at bikes
- Test out 3 different shapes

Another way of representing your goals is in a goal map, like this one:

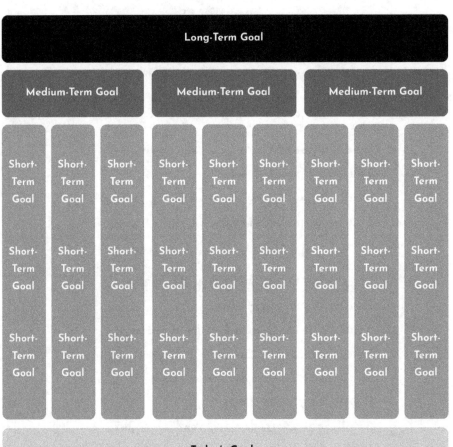

Instructions: Pick a business idea you have. Break it down into long-term, medium-term, and short-term goals. You can choose to do this exercise as a goal sheet or goal map.

Goal Sheet

Large goal:

Date to complete by:

- **Medium goal 1:**
  Date to complete by:
- **Medium goal 2:**
  Date to complete by:

⸻⸻⸻⸻⸻⸻

- Small goal 1.1:
  Date to complete by:
- Small goal 1.2:
  Date to complete by:
- Small goal 2.1:
  Date to complete by:
- Small goal 2.2:
  Date to complete by:
- Small goal 2.3:
  Date to complete by:

⸻⸻⸻⸻⸻⸻

Today's goals:

-
-
-
-

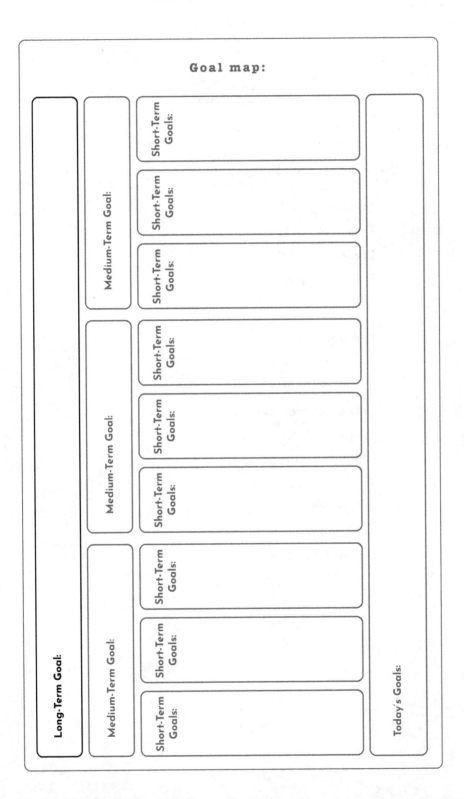

Goal map:

Long-Term Goal:

Medium-Term Goal:

Short-Term Goals:

Today's Goals:

CONCLUSION

Using goal sheets or goal maps is a great way to plan your solution and keep yourself on track. Keep it somewhere you can see it, and make sure you update it daily. There are many other ways to track your goals, so feel free to use any method that works for you. The important thing is keeping an eye on your goals, setting yourself deadlines, and making sure you're working toward them. Large goals are achieved by tackling small goals one step at a time.

CHAPTER 26

HACKING YOUR BRAIN

I t's time to hack your brain. This chapter will help you push your brain to become more creative and innovative. Whether you skipped ahead from earlier in the book or you've read through the entire process and are wondering what next, learning some hacking strategies will help you get the most out of your brain.

You need to push your brain—and yourself—to the absolute limit to continually ask more questions, identify more problems, and generate more creative and effective solutions in society and your life.

In this chapter, we'll look at six ways to inspire and push your brain to be more creative. They are:

1 Continually learning, including in areas where you're not an expert
2 Embracing the power of change, and having new experiences daily
3 Engaging in travel

4   Looking after yourself, including exercise, diet, and sleep

5   Thinking positively

6   Letting yourself be bored

ENGAGE IN CONTINUAL LEARNING

Until the day you die, you should never stop learning. The continual learning process will arm you with more information and more opportunities to identify ideas, so you can keep improving. Always spend a little of your time learning—learn what you're passionate about and keep taking in information. To keep learning, I like to create brain, heart, and hand diagrams. This is a visual way to lay out **what** you're learning (the brain), your **goal** for the learning (the heart), and **how** you're going to learn it (the hand).

EXERCISE 46: BRAIN, HEART, AND HAND

Instructions: Consider the next subject you want to learn about, and from that create your own brain, heart, and hand diagram. You can have multiple learning objectives—just use different colors for them.

Outcome: This is just one way to keep track of your learning. Keeping track of these areas will motivate you to actively pursue your learning goals and see your progress.

Read the news with targeted articles toward my goals
Use Spanish learning apps
Learn Spanish
Become more knowledgeable about the political climate
Learn C++
Take a 12-week online course
Become conversational
Be able to get a C++ certification
Be able to have intelligent discussions about states' rights, health care, and how the gov't impacts the economy

However, this is not the only way to keep track of learning goals. As long as you have a topic to learn about, you have a goal for what you want to accomplish, and you know how you want to get there, then you'll be on your way to achieving your learning goals.

The next step in the learning process is learning about things you're not an expert in. Exposing yourself to things you're not familiar with can be extremely helpful in the idea-finding process. Firstly, since you have little base knowledge, you'll enter the learning process without the same stigmas as an expert. The second major advantage is that you can take your expert knowledge from other areas and apply it to the field you're learning about. Think about the picture exercise you did earlier—combining two different things or solutions often leads to creative ideas.

Even though it might be harder to learn about areas you're not familiar with, the payoff in idea generation is exponential. Consider the 2017 *Vox* article titled "The man-made world is horribly designed. But copying nature helps." This article took a close look at the Japanese Shinkansen bullet train. Earlier iterations of the Japanese bullet train were round and loud, so inventors decided to change the shape by taking knowledge from a completely different area. An expert bird watcher, Eiji Nakatsu, redesigned the trains to be much quieter by mimicking three species of birds: the serrated wings of an owl, the rounded belly of the Adélie penguin, and the pointed beak of the Kingfisher. This new design was a success, and the train was much quieter.

EMBRACE CHANGE AND NEW THINGS

Change is a powerful tool in creating improvements and inspiring creativity. When you do the same thing or repeat the same process over and over again, you become immune to its potential problems, improvements, or insights. When you change your process or situation, your brain takes note of the new situation and becomes incredibly aware. It analyzes the potential places for improvement and increases in efficiency.

So, making your brain experience a different set of scenarios that you're not used to will ignite ideas, because you're seeing a different way of doing things. Every single change you make will help your brain develop and take in more information about the world. This might be a change in working location, your daily tasks, or the way you do something.

EXERCISE 47:

TIME FOR A

SIMPLE CHANGE

Instructions: Time for a change. Get up and move location now.

Outcome: Change is a powerful tool. Even small changes like this one can keep you on your toes and inspire creativity.

Another way to spark your brain is to give yourself new experiences every single day. It's important to constantly put yourself in new situations, because they'll not only expand your knowledge but also set your brain up to become aware of your surroundings and situations. This will stimulate ideas and solutions—the same as change.

Every morning, write down something you plan on doing differently that day. This might be something big like trying a new workout plan or visiting a new place, or something small like trying a new type of food or reading a new book.

EXERCISE 48:
NEW DAILY EXPERIENCES

Instructions: Write down what new daily experience you'll give yourself today, tomorrow, and the following day. Complete these experiences, then go back to take notes on anything new you noticed or thought about as a result.

Today:

_____

_____

_____

Tomorrow:

_____

_____

_____

The day after:

_____

_____

_____

Outcome: New experiences don't just inspire creativity—they make you happier overall. At the end of each day, you can reflect and say, "Hey, that's something new or different I did today!" Doing this means that your days, weeks, or even years won't blend together. It also helps you to avoid "gray days," where you repeatedly do the same thing over and over.

EMBRACE TRAVEL

Another great way to inspire new ideas and force your mind to think differently is through travel. Traveling can be done in many ways, and each can have a positive effect on you. There are four main types of travel:

1   Local travel
2   Regional travel
3   National travel
4   International travel

Local travel could be a bike trip to the next neighborhood or visiting a new part of your city or town. Experiencing or putting yourself in the travel mindset, even if it's a small trip, will inspire your creativity. Put yourself in the mindset that this is a mini-vacation, even if it's just for an hour or two. This kind of thinking makes you more likely to enjoy the moment and take in your surroundings.

Regional travel means taking a drive or a journey on public transportation that is farther than local travel but still within the region you live in within your country. This length of time means you should definitely be able to experience places you've never been to before, whether you're visiting a new museum or seeing how a different town operates. Regional travel enables you to get a fuller life perspective as you physically remove yourself from the places you normally go. This will inspire you and give you more knowledge and new experiences.

National travel means going to a place that is outside your region but within your own country. Generally, the farther you get from your home area, the more different daily life will be there. When you travel within your own country, you should start to notice some serious changes in how daily life is lived. Acknowledging these changes can inspire you to be part of the culture, learn from it, get new ideas, and see how things could be done differently.

International travel is traveling outside your own country, either via train, boat, plane, or another method. Each country does things differently, so by seeing other countries, you can learn a lot. Some of the best business ideas are inspired by appreciation for how people do things in other countries. If you can financially afford to do so, traveling internationally will really hack your brain. Immersing yourself in a new culture can be uncomfortable, but it can also provide a lifetime's worth of learning that will continue to inspire you.

EXERCISE 49:
PLAN A TRIP

Instructions: Take some time to plan out a trip—either big or small, national or international. Then follow through by going on the trip!

_____

_____

_____

_____

_____

Outcome: No matter how big or small, travel can inspire new ideas and help you see the world in a different light. It will inspire creativity and hack your brain to find new ideas.

LOOK AFTER YOUR BODY

It might seem strange to say, "look after your body" in a book about training your brain, but if you don't take care of your body, then your brain can't function optimally either. Sometimes, if you're struggling to come up with ideas or ask questions, it's because your body is tired, hungry, or not well.

To come up with creative ideas, you need to put your body in the best situation to set your brain up for success. To keep your brain in top format, you need to look after your body too, which means getting regular exercise, sleep, and good nutrition. If you're struggling in one of these areas and want to improve, a problem statement is a great place to start. You can use the processes in this book to come up with an idea to improve your health.

A recent journal study titled "The Impact of Physical Exercise on Convergent and Divergent Thinking" found that those who exercise or use bodily movements can overcome mental blocks and lack of inspiration (*Frontiers in Human Neuroscience*, 2013). Getting exercise is critical for your physical health, because it can improve your muscles and bones, increase your energy levels, reduce the risk of disease, and protect your heart, among many other benefits. However, it's also vital for your brain health, as exercise protects your memory, improves sleep quality, makes you feel happier, and reduces stress.

A 2014 study by *Harvard Business Review* also found that your diet can affect your creativity as "the more fruits and vegetables people consumed (up to seven portions per day), the happier, more engaged, and more creative they tended to be." Eating healthily can make you feel better both in body and mind, leading to improved energy levels and increased oxygen levels, both of which make our brains work better.

Likewise, research from Harvard University and Boston College found that getting the right amount of sleep improves creativity because "people seem to strengthen the emotional components of a memory during sleep, which may help spur the creative process." Sleep also results in improved memory, sharper attention, lower stress levels, less irritability, and clearer thinking.

THINK POSITIVELY

Positive thinking is another common brain hack. Being positive has many benefits, including improving your overall health, immunity, resilience, creativity, performance, and happiness levels—all of which will make you feel better both physically and mentally. It also reduces stress and helps you achieve your goals. Negative thoughts can weigh down your thinking, whereas having a free, positive, and open mind helps you come up with more creative and innovative ideas!

If you're struggling to be positive, here are some ways to improve your positivity:

- Do (or remind yourself of) the exercise on fundamental and daily happiness in chapter 18.
- Surround yourself with positive people. Your friends should be positive people who have a positive impact on your life. If they aren't, find friends who are positive.
- Engage in self-conversations that are uplifting. Being positive starts with being positive about yourself. Once you master being positive about yourself, everything else will fall into place.
- Start by changing your mindset and saying, "I can do this." Never say, "I'm not creative enough/good enough."
- Be kind and have gratitude for your life and what you have, which can also lead to more positivity.

A positive attitude is a choice. If you feel a lot of negative thoughts flowing in your head, take a step back and realize what's happening, like an out-of-body (or in this case "out-of-brain") experience. If you're a pessimist, changing yourself to become an optimist takes time. Ways of thinking can become hardwired into your brain. But keep at it the best you can. It might take months or even years to change your thinking.

A good way to keep track of your physical and mental wellness goals is a life triangle. This is an easy way to see how your goals relate to one another and how you plan to improve in these areas. Here, the triangle is split into the major areas we've just looked at: sleep, positivity, and exercise/diet, with an area to write your goals for each.

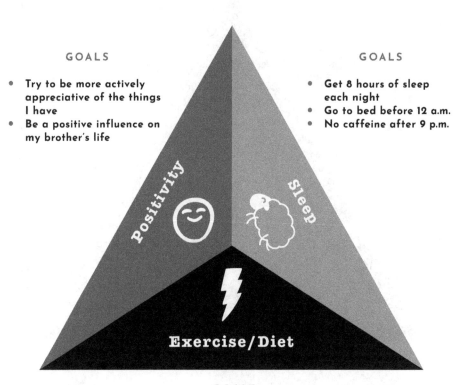

GOALS

- Try to be more actively appreciative of the things I have
- Be a positive influence on my brother's life

GOALS

- Get 8 hours of sleep each night
- Go to bed before 12 a.m.
- No caffeine after 9 p.m.

GOALS

- Work out at the gym and lift weights 3 days a week
- Lose 5 lbs. via a healthier diet

If maintaining a positive outlook feels overwhelming, consider seeing a mental health professional for support and options that might work for you to rewire your patterns of thinking. After all, taking care of your mind is just as important as taking care of your body.

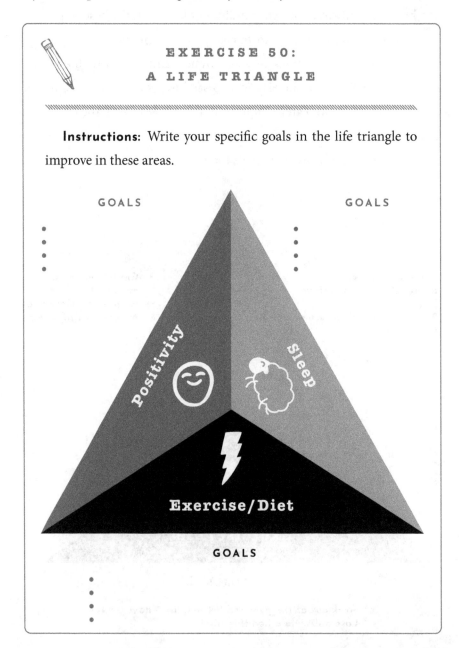

EXERCISE 50:
A LIFE TRIANGLE

Instructions: Write your specific goals in the life triangle to improve in these areas.

GOALS   GOALS

Positivity   Sleep

Exercise/Diet

GOALS

LET YOURSELF BE BORED

When was the last time you were bored? Think about it. Every time we feel bored, we immediately pick up our phones, respond to texts, or check social media. Was there a time when you were actually bored and had *nothing to do?* No phone, no TV, no video games, no internet? To help with the creative process, you should let yourself be bored more often!

What happens when you let yourself be bored? If you don't pick up your phone or immediately try to fix your boredom, your mind will begin to entertain you. It forces your brain to roam and think about things. You'll begin to tackle problems or subjects in your head. Your mind begins to wander to faraway places. Your imagination is sparked. A lot of creativity can happen when you're bored, so we humans need to be bored more often!

EXERCISE 51:
BE BORED

Instructions: For three days, every time you feel bored, don't check your social media, pick up your phone, turn on the TV, or use any other technology. Just let yourself be bored, and see where your mind goes.

Outcome: This task is hard! Even for just three days. Our phones and social media form habits and become addictive. However, if you can step back and let yourself be bored, your mind will thank you with a ton of creativity, and you'll be able to generate astronomically more ideas! If you're interested in learning more, Manoush Zomorodi talks about boredom as a catalyst to creative thinking in her fantastic TED Talk: "How Boredom Can Lead to Your Most Brilliant Ideas."

CONCLUSION

As you can see, techniques to spark creativity abound, and you may not have considered all of them. To come up with new ideas, it's important to engage in continual learning—both in the areas you're skilled in and those where you're not an expert. You also need to actively make changes, experience new things, and engage in travel, and these subtle shifts will force your brain to become more aware of its surroundings.

To train your brain, you need to look after your body, including your diet, exercise, and sleep—as your brain only functions at its best when your body is taken care of. You also need to think positively and be nice to yourself, because positive thinking leads to more creative ideas.

If you read this chapter after chapter 6, then go back and continue reading—I also suggest you read this chapter again when you come to it to reinforce your creativity!

CHAPTER 27

A RUN·THROUGH
OF THE ENTIRE
PROCESS

Y ou now have all of the tools necessary to start coming up with more ideas than you ever thought possible, and ones that are actually viable! In this chapter, we'll run through the entire process from square one using our character Mae as an example. We'll take all of the steps so you can see how an idea develops.

HOW AN IDEA DEVELOPS

Mae was on her way to work when she got a call from her friend Olivia. Olivia was extremely tired and had a long drive to work, so she asked whether Mae would be willing to chat throughout the journey to help her stay awake. Mae gladly accepted, since she was on public transport and had nothing to do anyway. They talked for 30 minutes until Olivia arrived at work.

Mae knew that driving tired was dangerous, but she wondered how dangerous **(The Question "How?")**. She did a quick internet search and found that thousands of crashes are caused by driving fatigue each year, as reported by the police according to the National Highway and Traffic Safety Administration. She also found that 60 percent of adult drivers had driven a vehicle while drowsy in the previous year, according to a 2005 Sleep in America poll.

Clearly, driving tired was a problem, but Mae wondered why there were so many people who were willing to drive tired **(Why?)**. She began to dig deeper **(The Why 3x Rule)**. She discovered that the government doesn't have any rules against driving tired. But, why? She tried to answer her own question: "Well, maybe it's hard to create a rule against something we can't measure." This led her to the question: "Why can't we measure tiredness?"

She found that there was not a good way to measure tiredness. So, she began to ask more questions such as, "What skills are important in driving?" She came up with the answers: focus and attention **(Asking Questions)**. Before considering the solution, she looked at what stigmas she had about the situation and began writing them down. First, she used the blank-paper approach for her problem **(Stigma Strategies)**. She started with a couple of stigmas she had:

- The solution has to be a part of the car.
- It has to be something people will use.
- It would always need to be active.

She went on to analyze those stigmas and decided that her solution doesn't need to necessarily be a part of the car. She decided that "drowsy drivers will need to interact with the solution" is a requirement, not a stigma. If the solution doesn't have any interaction with drowsy drivers, then it won't solve the problem. She decided that her solution doesn't need to always be active, because it might not necessarily need to analyze tiredness the entire time that someone is driving **(Erasing Stigmas)**.

Then she moved on to the solution process and began brainstorming and making a mind map as follows **(Brainstorming and Mind Mapping):**

Her mind map generated lots of options. After looking at these options, she selected three:

- An eye scanner that will scan the driver's eyes to measure tiredness
- An app that plays two minutes of games to test the driver's attention and reaction time against a baseline
- A car test that will rate how tired the driver is based on the first five minutes of their driving

She then took these ideas through the feasibility check and realized she needed more information on certain points. After some research and calls, she found that some car companies are interested in helping to make their cars safer **(Is There a Market for the Idea?)**. She also found that they want it now, as people are dying every day from this issue **(Does the Market Want It Now?)**. Then she asked herself whether she had the resources to make it a reality. She wasn't a scientist, but she was a coder. She decided that she didn't have the resources to make this happen, so she wanted to bring on a sleep science expert as a partner.

Then she decided to share her idea with some potential customers via an online forum on driver safety **(Share, Share, Share)**. The idea that got the most positive reviews was the app with two minutes of games. She continued her market research and got feedback that she should also include visuomotor skills. So, she went back and adjusted her app to measure the driver's focus, reaction time, and visuomotor skills. During the feedback stage, she also received a suggestion that it should link to the car's system. After she adjusted the idea, she ran it through the feasibility check again.

Her final solution was an app that links to the car and makes the driver play 120 seconds of games to test their focus, reaction time, and visuomotor skills against the person's baseline to help start the car.

As you can see, this is just one example of how an idea goes through the process to become a creative solution to a common problem.

EXERCISE 52:

THE FULL RUN-THROUGH

Instructions: Practice running through the entire process for a problem, question, or idea you have. If it's easier, you can start with a simple problem and then try again with a more complex one. Remember to go through the process of:

1   Identifying a problem, need, or want
2   Asking questions
3   Finding and erasing stigmas
4   Coming up with ideas for a possible solution
5   Doing a feasibility check
6   Sharing the idea with others
7   Making a plan of action

If you get stuck, you can go back to the information in the individual section you're stuck on. Also feel free to go backward in the process—it's hard to get everything perfect on the first try.

CONCLUSION

The more you practice this process, the better you'll get at it. Keep doing it—and you'll soon become an idea-developing master! For now, you don't need to actually take the ideas forward and bring them to reality. The point is to train your brain to naturally do this process.

CHAPTER 28

MAKE IT
HAPPEN

ow it's time to bring together everything you've learned and start making it happen in your life. In this chapter, we'll review the key points in the process:

1 Start by identifying your problems, needs, and wants—or those around you.

    Remember to look out for the magic words you hear, such as "hate" and "annoy."

2 Ask questions about everything, as this can help you identify problems, needs, and wants, and ask more questions.

    Remember to ask "Why 3x" to get to the root of an issue or problem.

3 If you're having trouble coming up with problems, needs, and wants, look at your environment.

    Sometimes, working backward by looking at already-created solutions can help you identify problems, needs, and wants more effectively.

4   Next, you need to find your stigmas about the problem, need, or want.

Use the stigma-finding exercises to identify any stigmas you have.

5   When you've found your stigmas, make them a requirement for the solution or erase them.

To check whether a stigma is a requirement, try the wild-imagination strategy, the blank-paper approach, and the alien-invasion strategy.

6   After you've erased your stigmas, brainstorm possible ideas.

Remember to use mind maps, and don't discard those crazy ideas!

7   Start turning your ideas into possible solutions by putting them through a feasibility check.

Remember the key questions for personal life: Do you want to pursue it? Do you value it? Does it make you happy? What are the pros and cons? Do you have the resources?

Remember the key questions for business life: Is there a market for it? Does the market want it now? Do you have the resources?

8   Next, you need to share your idea and get feedback on it from others.

Remember to see all feedback as an opportunity to improve the solution.

9   Plan the solution, and break it down into smaller goals.

Use a notebook to track your goals and progress, and work on them every day.

10   Make sure you bring your ideas to reality!

When you've come up with a solution, don't just file it away—bring it to life.

If you get stuck, hack your brain. Sometimes, simple actions can open up your mind to more ideas.

Additionally, in case you need a reminder, here's the Your Big Idea journey map:

1 START

➤➤ I'm ready to go ....GO TO 2

2 ASK QUESTIONS AND IDENTIFY PROBLEMS, NEEDS, AND WANTS

➤➤ I have completed asking questions, discovering, and have identified a problem, need, or want............GO TO 3

3 FIND AND ERASE STIGMAS (USE STIGMA-FINDING AND ERASING STRATEGIES)

➤➤ I still don't have a good enough understanding of my problem, need, or want to find and erase stigmas...................GO TO 2

➤➤ I have found and erased stigmas and I am ready for brainstorming and mind mapping.....................GO TO 4

4 BRAINSTORMING AND MIND MAPPING

➤➤ I have brainstormed and I need to go back to the drawing board based on my results..................GO TO 2

➤➤ I need to go back and relook at finding and identifying my stigmas................................GO TO 3

➤➤ I have brainstormed and I am ready to move forward to a solution.................................GO TO 5

5 COMBINE AND SELECT SOLUTIONS

➤➤ I need to go back and brainstorm further to get the best solutions..............................GO TO 4

➤➤ I have my solution! ....GO TO 6

6 THREE-PART FEASIBILITY CHECK

➤➤ After completing my feasibility check, I realize this is not feasible ....GO TO 2

➤➤ After completing my feasibility check, I realize I need to re-evaluate my stigmas.................GO TO 3

➤➤ After completing my feasibility check, I need to re-evaluate my idea...................................GO TO 4

➤➤ After completing my feasibility check, I need to relook at the solution I selected.....................GO TO 5

➤➤ My idea passes the feasibility check...............................GO TO 7

7 SHARE

➤➤ After talking to people, I need to go back to the drawing board.................................GO TO 2

➤➤ After talking to people, I need to re-evaluate my stigmas...........GO TO 3

➤➤ After talking to people, I need to go back to my brainstorming stage..................................GO TO 4

➤➤ After talking to people, I need to relook at my feasibility check.................................GO TO 6

➤➤ I am ready to go!.................GO TO 8

8 YOUR NEXT BIG IDEA! IT'S TIME TO MOVE FORWARD.

EXERCISE 53:
IDEAS 1-100

Instructions: Now, it's time to challenge yourself! Use the strategies you've learned to keep your brain alert and put your learning into practice. Next, you'll find a list of 1–100 empty spaces. Come up with 100 ideas, just like the class assignment I mentioned at the beginning of the book.

Remember that all problems have multiple idea solutions. If you can identify 10–20 problems and take five minutes to brainstorm each of them, you'll be able to reach the magical 100 ideas. It may take a couple of weeks, but if you stay focused, you *will* get there—and you'll notice more opportunities and ideas than you ever imagined were possible.

This could be the first of many 100-ideas lists!

1 _____

2 _____

3 _____

4 _____

5 _____

6 _____

7 _____

8 _____

9

10

11

12

13

14

15

16

17

18

19

20

21

22

23

24

25

26

27 _____

28 _____

29 _____

30 _____

31 _____

32 _____

33 _____

34 _____

35 _____

36 _____

37 _____

38 _____

39 _____

40 _____

41 _____

42 _____

43 _____

44
_____

45
_____

46
_____

47
_____

48
_____

49
_____

50
_____

51
_____

52
_____

53
_____

54
_____

55
_____

56
_____

57
_____

58
_____

59
_____

60
_____

61

62

63

64

65

66

67

68

69

70

71

72

73

74

75

76

77

78 _____

79 _____

80 _____

81 _____

82 _____

83 _____

84 _____

85 _____

86 _____

87 _____

88 _____

89 _____

90 _____

91 _____

92 _____

93 _____

94 _____

95	
96	
97	
98	
99	
100	

CONCLUSION

While this process may seem challenging at first, the more you practice, the more natural it will become. Soon you'll find yourself being able to go through the entire process multiple times a day!

CHAPTER 29

WHAT NEXT?

As time passes, some of the lessons in this book may get foggy, you may forget some things, or you may fall out of the good habits you've built. It's important that the skills you build aren't lost. Practicing is an important part of keeping your brain in top shape. Taking five minutes on your way to work or whenever you can to practice this style of thinking—noticing opportunities or working on problems—can allow this thinking style to be impactful and change the way you think. But a change in thinking doesn't happen overnight.

Don't just put your notebook away and stop thinking about your new-found processes for growing and testing your ideas. Your notebook should be a reminder to constantly think of ideas. You should never stop the thinking process, and seeing a list on your phone or in your notebook can jolt your mind into the idea-finding state.

It's important to regularly evaluate your life and put your ideas into action. If it's an idea with work, then tell your boss, or even better, start a business. There is no "right time" to take a risk, so if you have an idea you're passionate about and that you think is viable, don't let it go. You can accomplish your goals.

Do it now!

EXERCISE 54:
ONE-MONTH CHALLENGE

Every day for one month, spend time thinking about the concepts in this book and applying them to your everyday life. If you can do that, you'll have formed a habit of creating ideas and finding solutions. It's not going to be easy, because your brain will want to revert to what it's comfortable with, but if you want your mind to start being naturally creative, then it takes practice. Practice is the only way to make a change for life. You've made it this far, so I know you can take the steps to practice and train your brain long after you've finished reading this book!

JOIN OUR ONLINE SOCIAL GROUPS

Because sharing ideas is such an important part of the process, there are Facebook and LinkedIn groups dedicated to it, titled "Your Next Big Idea," where you can interact with other readers, share your ideas, and talk about your progress:

- **Facebook:** facebookgroup.yournextbigideabook.com
- **LinkedIn:** linkedingroup.yournextbigideabook.com

This is a positive community to help push your ideas forward, where you can test ideas and find accountability with a group of people trying to improve their idea processes too. Feel free to use the hashtags #my100ideas, #mynextbigidea, and #yournextbigidea on Facebook as well as Instagram, Twitter, or LinkedIn to share your progress publicly.

CONCLUSION

Now, after reading this book, do you think you can come up with 100 ideas a week? Are you skeptical? Honestly? I mean *100 ideas a week?* That sounded pretty crazy 28 chapters ago.

It may have seemed crazy at first, but now that you have the skills to make this crazy concept your reality, it's time to come up with your next big idea!

CONGRATULATIONS AND THANK YOU!

ongratulations! You made it through the book. It may seem like a simple feat, but often it's the small things in life that get you closer to your goals. Make sure you reward yourself. This book is the first step in thinking creatively, innovatively, and in a way you never imagined before.

Lastly, I want to say thank you! Taking the time to read through an author's work takes commitment, especially when that book specifically aims to challenge your thinking. So, thank you for sticking with it. More importantly, thank you for becoming part of a community where you could be a massive opportunity-finder or solution-provider, because these are the types of people who have a real impact on the world.

CPSIA information can be obtained
at www.ICGtesting.com
Printed in the USA
BVHW081002240421
605735BV00009B/1664